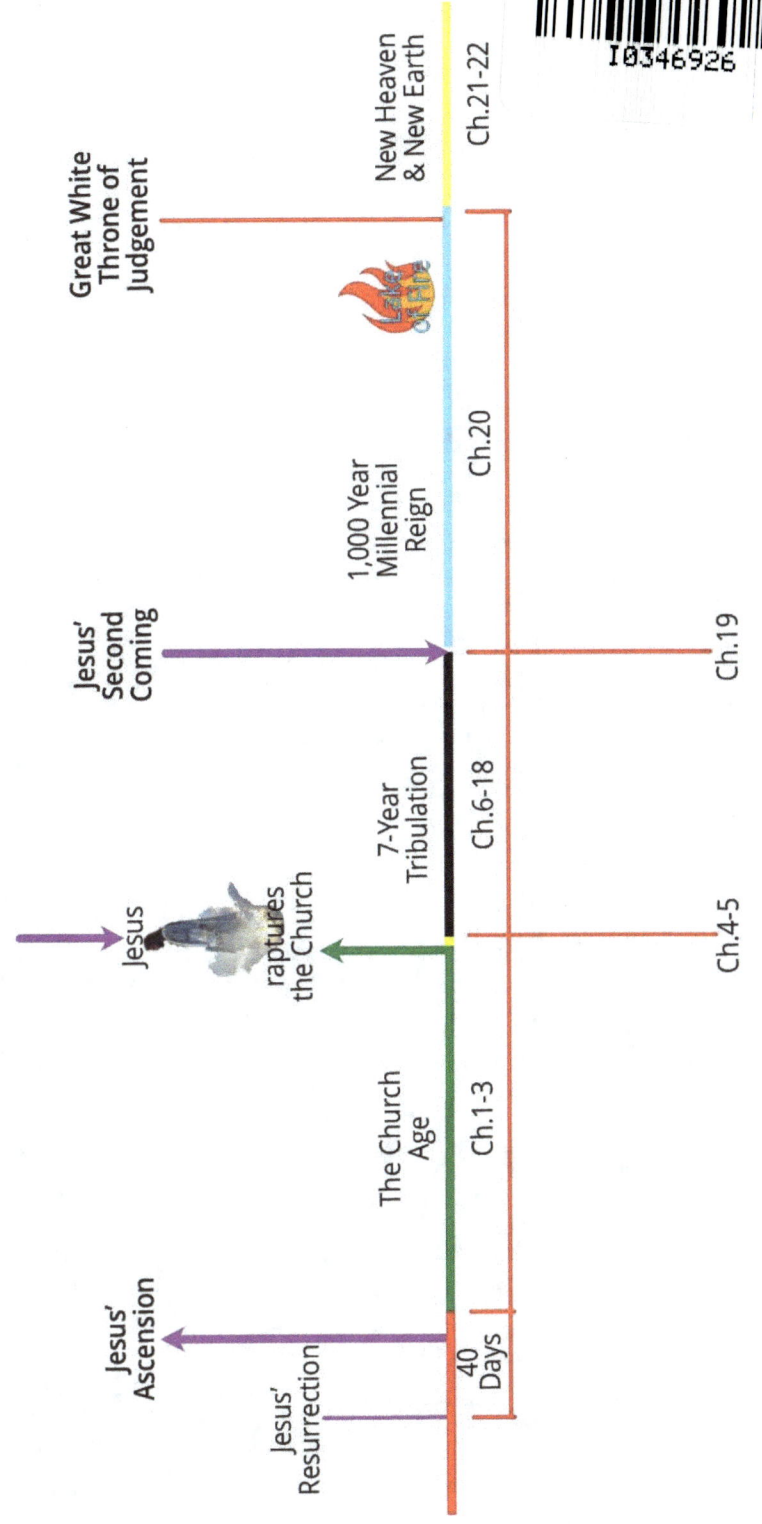

The Book of **Revelation**

Simply Put

by
Barbara Jackson

The Book of Revelation

Author: Barbara Jackson

Copyright © 2025 Barbara Jackson

The author asserts the moral right to be identified as the author of this work.

The right of Barbara Jackson to be identified as author of this work has been asserted by the author in accordance with section 77 and 78 of the Copyright, Designs and Patents Act 1988.

First Published in 2025

ISBN 978-1-83538-633-0 (Paperback)
978-1-83538-634-7 (E-Book)

Book cover design by Barbara Jackson

Book layout by:
    Lawrence Jackson & Maple Publishers
    www.maplepublishers.com

Published by:
    Maple Publishers
    Fairbourne Drive, Atterbury,
    Milton Keynes,
    MK10 9RG, UK
    www.maplepublishers.com

Unless otherwise indicated, all Scripture quotations are taken from the Holy Bible, New Living Translation, copyright 1996. Used by permission of Tyndale House Publishers, Inc., Wheaton, Illinois 60189. All rights reserved.

A CIP catalogue record for this title is available from the British Library.

All rights reserved. No part of this book may be reproduced or translated in any form or by any means, electronic or mechanical, including photocopying, recording or by any information storage and retrieval system without written permission from the author.

Acknowledgements

I am indebted to my dear husband, Lawrence, without whose help this book would never have made it into print. He has diligently typed and laid out this book and also produced most of the graphics. He has borne, with patience and no complaint, the countless rewrites, revisions and amendments, which have been a necessary part of compiling the book.

My thanks go to all who have encouraged me in the writing of this book. A special mention needs to be made of Gilian Thomas and Yvonne Gil, who have given up an extraordinary amount of their time to proof read and edit my book. I am enormously grateful to these two friends.

I also wish to thank

> Derek Walker for his kind permission to use his Church Era Timeline; and

> James Park for his kind permission to use his graphic of the statue in Nebuchadnezzar's dream.

Contents

	Page
Introduction	i
Setting the Scene	ii
A brief synopsis of each chapter	iv
Chapter 1 — John meets the risen Jesus, Who gives him the revelation	1
Chapters 2 & 3 — The Church of Jesus Christ	4
Diagram showing the seven churches of Revelation	5
Map 1 shows the location of the seven churches to whom John wrote his letters	6
The Rapture	15
Chapter 4 — The Church in Heaven	16
Chapter 5 — Jesus alone has the legal right to open the scroll	19
Map 2 shows the extent of the land covenanted by God to Abraham, Isaac, Jacob and their descendants	20
Map 3 shows the land distribution between the 12 tribes of Judah	21
Overview of the Tribulation	24
The Judgements	26
Chapter 6 — Judgements of the Seals	27
Chapter 7 — The Interlude and Beyond	29
Chapter 8 — Judgements of Trumpets 1-4	32
The Counterfeit Trinity	35

Contents (continued)

Chapter 9	Judgements of Trumpets 5-6 (Woes 1-2)	36
Chapter 10	An Interlude (which continues into chapters 11 & 12)	40
Chapter 11	The 2 Witnesses and the 3rd Woe	43
Chapter 12	The Woman, the Son and the Dragon	46
Chapter 13	Opposition to God's Redemptive Plan	50
Chapter 14	Harvesting the Nations	53
	Map 4 shows the position of Edom and Megiddo	56
Chapter 15	Setting the scene for the last 7 Judgements	57
Chapter 16	Judgements of the 7 Bowls	59
Chapter 17	Babylon 1: Destruction of the Harlot	62
Chapter 18	Babylon 2: Final Destruction of Babylon	65
Chapter 19	Jesus' Second Coming	67
Chapter 20	The Millennium	70
Chapter 21	The New Jerusalem	75
Chapter 22	It is finished	79
Appendix 1	Jesus' Olivet Discourse	84
Appendix 2	The Relevance of the Book of Daniel to the Book of Revelation	87
Glossary		99
Bibliography		102
Video Teaching		102

Introduction

Several of my friends commented to me that they found the Book of Revelation complex and difficult to understand. After praying about this, I sensed that God was calling me to write a simple commentary about it, so I made a detailed study of it. I hope that this resulting book will be easy for anyone to use and understand.

Since this book is designed to be used as a simple commentary, it needs to be read alongside the Bible.

There are many views regarding the meaning of the Book of Revelation. I have tried to stick to views held by the majority of the Evangelical Church and, where different interpretations are given, I leave it to you to choose whichever sits best with yourself. I am using the futuristic form of prophetic interpretation (i.e. the belief that the bulk of the prophecy will take place in the future).

The style of this book varies from chapter to chapter but my aim has been to make the text for each chapter as clear as possible. Sometimes I use notes, sometimes prose, but mostly notes verse by verse.

On a practical level, the chapter numbers in this book relate to the equivalent chapter numbers in the Book of Revelation. In some places, John moves backwards and forwards in time, so the Book of Revelation is not quite written in chronological order. Any background information or references that I think might be helpful are included as standalone pages and appendices.

A dagger symbol (†) following a word denotes that the meaning of that word is to be found in the Glossary (page 99).

Setting the Scene

The Book of Revelation is comprised of a series of prophetic visions† that were given to the apostle John when he was exiled on the island of Patmos between AD 86 and AD 96. Patmos is off the coast of Asia Minor (modern day Turkey).

This short commentary aims to guide the reader through a basic study of the Book of Revelation.

The first three chapters of Revelation are easy to understand as they deal with the Church from the time of its conception, after the first day of Pentecost, until Jesus comes again for His Church at the Rapture†.

In chapter 4 we see the Church raptured and in heaven, represented by the 24 Elders.

So what of the rest? God promised Abraham in the Book of Genesis that, through him, all nations† of the world would be blessed (Genesis 17:1-8). The time of the Gentiles will have largely been in the Church Age (see the Time Line at the beginning of this book). So what about Abraham's descendants, the Jews?

We need to realise that the Jews have always been God's chosen people because of the faith of Abraham. King David's love for God, cemented Jesus' line of descent.

When Jesus came to earth the first time, the Jewish leaders rejected Him as their Messiah. However, God did not withdraw from the covenant He had made with Abraham or stop loving His chosen people.

Chapters 5 to 19 explain the battle between God, Who wants to save His people once and for all, and Satan, who wants to destroy all Jews. An evangelistic crusade by Messianic Jews (Jews who have become Christians) will kick start proceedings and both Jews and Gentiles will respond and receive Jesus as their Saviour. These chapters refer to the time of the Tribulation†. This is a period of 7 years when life on earth will be more difficult than at any other time in history.

†See Glossary

During the Tribulation, God's first strategy is to withdraw His protection from the earth. After that, more severe judgements follow and Satan does his worst. Finally, all Jews turn to Jesus as their Messiah.

Having accomplished the total salvation of the Jewish nation, Jesus is victorious over Satan and all of Israel's enemies. Jesus establishes His kingdom on earth for 1,000 years and He governs from the City of Jerusalem. All believers will be part of the governance of the city.

When the thousand years come to an end, Satan is released from his imprisonment in the abyss so that the remaining inhabitants on earth can choose whom they wish to follow: Jesus or Satan.

Lastly, a new heaven and earth appear and a new city of Jerusalem. All of God's people – Christian Jews and Gentiles of all nations – can now live for eternity in an intimate relationship with their Father, through His Son, Jesus, the Lamb of God.

A summary of each chapter follows.

A brief synopsis of each chapter in the Book of Revelation

Chapter	
1	John meets the risen Jesus, Who gives him the prophetic revelation.
2-3	Jesus' messages to the 7 churches.
4	In a vision, John is transported to heaven.
5	Jesus, the Lamb, is the only one worthy to open the scroll of the Title Deeds of the Earth.
6	Jesus opens the first 6 seals, at which point God begins to relinquish His protection over the earth. (The Tribulation begins.)
7	144,000 Jews from the 12 tribes of Israel are marked with God's seal of protection so that they are ready to spearhead a worldwide evangelistic campaign. (Although it is not mentioned here, this is the same starting time for the 2 witnesses, who begin their mission on the Holy Mountain in front of the 3rd Temple.)
	SILENCE, WHICH DENOTES JUDGEMENT TO COME
8	After the Ominous Silence, Jesus opens the 7th seal, which invokes the 1st Trumpet to sound. The 1st Trumpet heralds serious judgements that are to come upon the earth.
9	The 1st Woe is that of demons, which look a bit like locusts and are allowed to harm animal life for 5 months. They do not kill but their sting is so painful that some people will wish they could die. The 6th Trumpet marks the half-way point of the Tribulation. The 2nd Woe brings a cavalry of demons, who do kill. One third of the world's population will die.
10	A mighty angel hands a small scroll to John. After he has read it he is not allowed to divulge its contents but has to eat it. It tastes sweet but feels sour in his stomach.

Chapter	
11	The site of the new 3rd Temple is measured. The 2 prophets (Moses and Elijah) witness about Jesus. After 3½ years the beast kills them. (At this time the prophets' testimony is complete.) After 3½ days of their bodies lying in the streets of Jerusalem, they rise from the dead and are called up into heaven. The 7th Trumpet is blown, heralding the 3rd Woe and containing all the judgements of the 7 bowls. There is great rejoicing in heaven because God is moving and the end is in sight.
12	The woman, representing Israel, gives birth to a son (Jesus), whom the dragon (Satan) tries to destroy. However, during mid-Tribulation, Israel flees to the wilderness where she is protected during the 2nd half of the Tribulation.
13	A beast comes out of the sea. This beast's horns represent the Gentile nations who, throughout history, have waged war on Israel. The 7th head represents the Antichrist, who persecutes Jews and Christians. The beast, who comes out of the earth, is the false prophet. His powers are from Satan and he witnesses† to people about the beast of the sea (the Antichrist†).
14	The interlude which has been to enable Jews and Christians to escape, has ended. The 144,000 are a special offering to God. Angels are dispatched to: • preach the Gospel • foretell the fall of Babylon • condemn those following the Beast • announce the wheat harvest • hold the sharp sickle for harvesting the grapes
15	The scene is set for the last 7 judgements (the bowls). This time period starts the last 3½ years of the Tribulation. The judgements of the bowls are very severe, in a last ditch attempt by God to convince mankind to turn to Him, Satan is allowed to do his worst.
16	The 7 bowls of wrath are poured out. The troops start to gather at the Hill of Megiddo.
17	This chapter relates to spiritual Babylon. The pseudo religion (the harlot†) is destroyed by the beast (the Antichrist) because she has served her purpose in enabling the beast to have total political and economic power.
18	This chapter announces the destruction of Babylon. This world power has killed so many of God's people that streets run with their blood. The millstone predicts the final demise of Babylon.

Chapter	
19	After much praise in heaven for the avenging of the martyrs, the bride of Christ is made ready to go with Jesus as He prepares to do battle with His enemies at the Battle of Armageddon†. The beast (the Antichrist) and the false prophet are thrown into the Lake of Fire.
20	Satan is bound and locked in the bottomless pit for 1,000 years, the period of Jesus' millennial reign on earth. After this, Satan is released and he seeks out the people who would prefer to follow him than to follow Jesus. This is important because only then will all of mankind have been given the choice between following Jesus and following Satan. Finally, all who have rebelled against Jesus will be judged and both they and Satan will be cast into the Lake of Fire.
21	The New Jerusalem is seen in all its splendour. It is a most beautiful, colourful place needing no light because the glory of God is its light. There will be no more pain, sorrow or tears.
22	The source of water for the New Jerusalem is a clear river flowing from the throne of God. A Tree (or Trees) of Life grows on each side of the river giving a fresh crop of fruit each month. The book ends with final messages from John that he has received this prophecy from the God Who spoke to the Old Testament prophets. Jesus tells us that He is coming soon.

†See Glossary

The Commentary

The Book of Revelation
Chapter 1
John meets the risen Jesus, Who gives him the revelation

Commentary on chapter 1

John was on the island of Patmos, where he had been exiled by the Roman Governor, Domitian, for preaching the Gospel. John was worshipping God one Sunday when he had a vision of Jesus, Who gave him this revelation, or series of prophecies†, about the future.

Verses 4 and 11 John is writing to the seven churches in Asia: Ephesus, Smyrna, Pergamon, Thyatira, Sardius, Philadelphia and Laodicea, to tell them what he saw.

John was told that anyone who reads the prophecies in the Book of Revelation and obeys its teaching will be blessed.

Verses 4-6 The book begins with a message of grace and peace from the apostle John to the seven churches. The message enclosed in this book is authorised by God the Father, the Son and the Holy Spirit. Jesus is hailed as:
- the faithful witness
- the first to be resurrected from the dead
- the King or Ruler over all

Jesus is the author of our salvation through His death on the cross, while the Sevenfold Spirit is the Holy Spirit.

Verse 7 John sees Jesus returning to earth at His Second Coming when everyone on earth sees Him, including those who rejected and crucified Him during His earthly ministry over 2,000 years ago. They will all mourn and wail for what they did to Him.

†See Glossary

| Verse 12 | 1 | The seven golden lamp stands represent the seven churches. Seven is the number of spiritual completeness and the lamp stands represent the whole church both then and throughout history. |
| Verse 13 | 2 | The resurrected Jesus is standing in their midst. |

    a. He is wearing a long robe – the Jewish high priests wore long robes.

    b. He has a golden sash across His chest – gold represents great authority.

Verses 14-15

    c. His hair is white – white light signifies the glory of God which is shining from Jesus.

    d. His eyes are like flames of fire – nothing escapes His vision.

    e. His feet are like polished bronze – bronze denotes judgement.

    f. His voice thunders.

Verse 16

    g. He has seven stars in His hand – the stars are pastors of the seven churches. (*Angelos* means messenger or pastor.)

    h. He has a two-edged sword in His mouth (c.f. Hebrews 4:12 where the writer says that the Word of God is living and powerful and sharper than any two-edged sword).

The sword – or *Word of God* – is used to instruct, discipline, train, divide good from bad, etc.

    i. His face is like strong sunshine – this speaks of His divine glory (cf. the transfiguration Matthew 17:2).

Verse 17	j. He is the Alpha and Omega – the beginning and the end.
Verse 18	k. He has the keys to Hades and death so we have nothing to fear from them.

Summary

The picture we get of Jesus in chapter 1 is that:

- He is the greatest high priest of all time. He has total authority and shines with the glory of God.
- He is all seeing, so nothing escapes his attention and He has a voice which cannot be ignored.
- He wants to be a shepherd to the pastors of the 7 churches John mentions and also to pastors throughout history. He also wants to teach and, when necessary, discipline the pastors with His Word, both then and throughout history.
- He is the beginning and the end and has defeated both death and hell. Therefore, we and the pastors need not fear. Jesus is now waiting for history to work out God's purposes before He returns.

The Book of Revelation
Chapter 2 and 3
The Church of Jesus Christ

Introduction to John's letters and the Church Eras

Chapters 2 and 3 record John's letters to the churches at Ephesus, Smyrna, Pergamos, Thyatira, Sardis, Philadelphia and Laodicea. These towns were situated in the east of modern day Turkey (see Map 1).

Each of the 7 individual churches that Jesus asked John to write to, held some views that were different from the others. The letters are directed to the 'messengers', i.e. pastors, of the churches.

In addition to there being 7 actual churches that John wrote to, there are also 7 Church Eras that are periods of time, each church representing one era. The present church age is still in one of those eras. Each Church Era is the representation of the church as an institution at that particular time in our church history (see diagram opposite).

The institution of the church in each era had/has similar faults and/or blessings to the church it is named after.

The institution of the church is defined by the beliefs, rules and regulations that govern it. Churches in different eras held some different views from each other. In most eras, except the first, some of the beliefs taught to lay people veered away from Biblical truth.

Within each institutional church era there have always been individual true Christians who believe that their salvation and reconciliation to God are purely down to Jesus' sacrificial death, as opposed to having to earn their salvation through obeying man-made rules and doing 'good deeds' which, of course, the Bible says is impossible.

> But we are all as an unclean thing, and all our righteousnesses are as filthy rags. (Isaiah 64:6 AV)

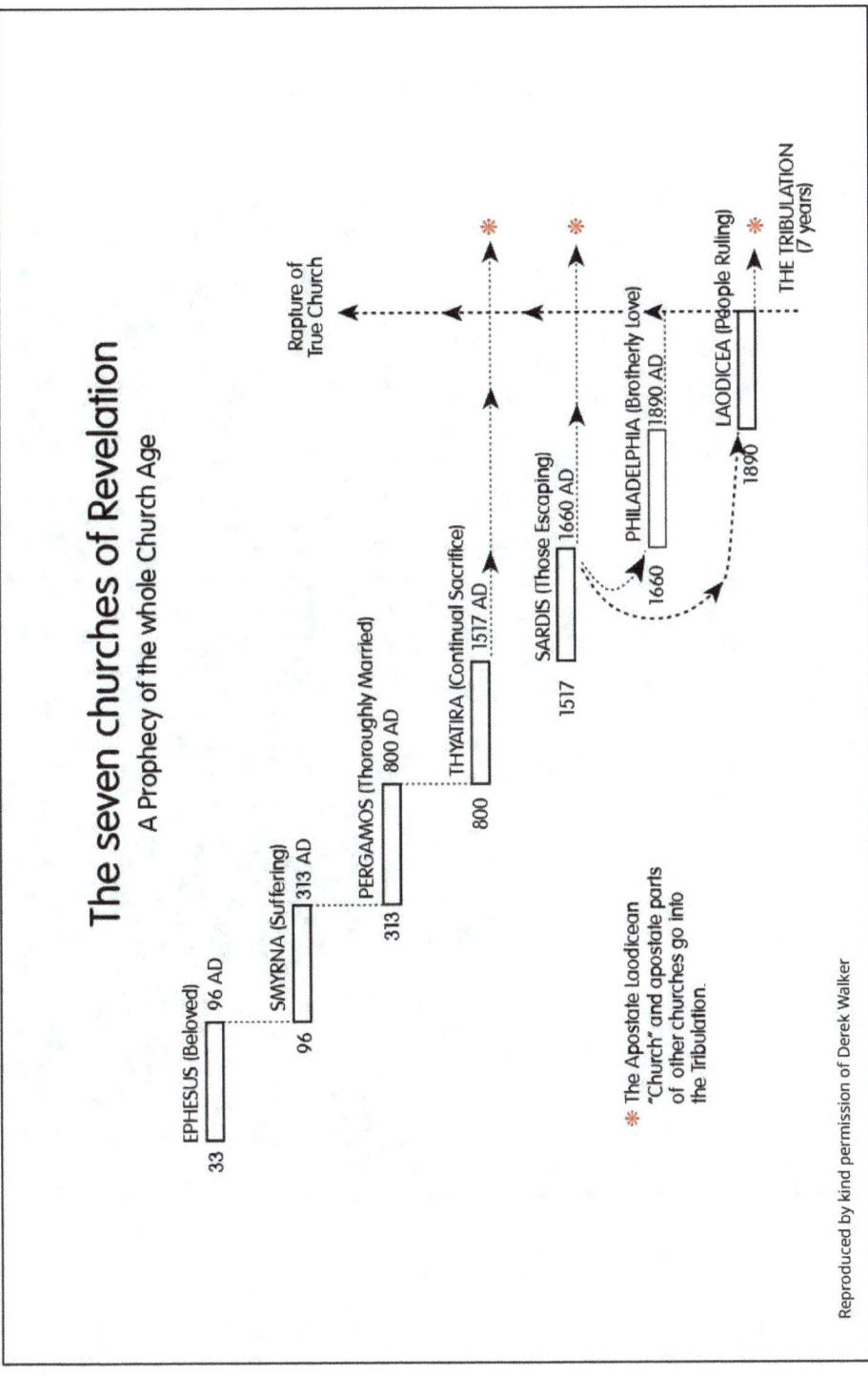

Map 1 shows the location of the seven churches to whom John wrote his letters

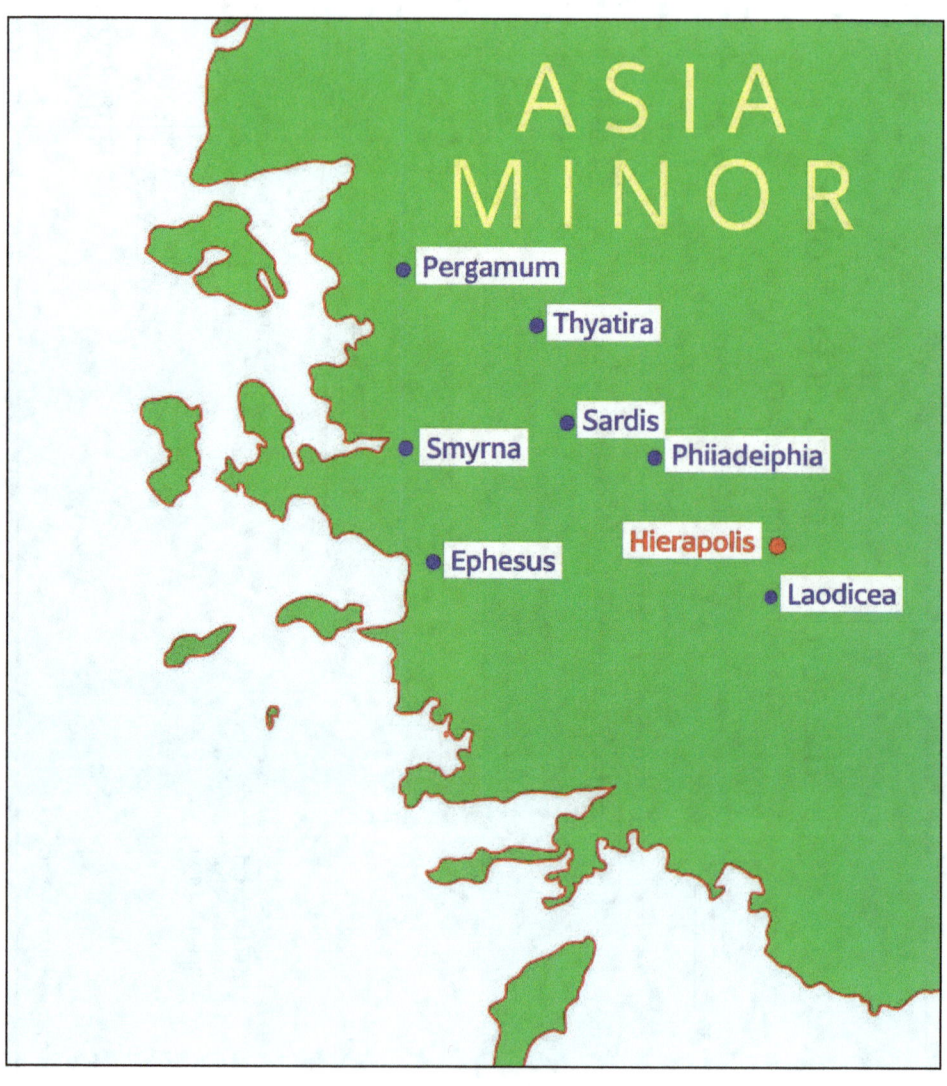

*Asia Minor is present-day Turkey

Letters to the Seven Churches

Commentary on Chapter 2

1 *EPHESUS* (Verses 1-7)   *Era Date: AD 33–96*

   Church Name Meaning: Desired, beloved

   - The church at Ephesus represents the church of the 1st century: the Apostolic Church†.
   - First generation Christians were vibrant witnesses because of their loving relationship with Jesus.
   - Second generation Christians had some problems:
     1. Their love of the Lord had begun to fade but they were still faithful and practised sound Bible-based teaching.
     2. They resisted false teachings but the first-love of the first generation had faded and their witnessing had become more of an obligation.
     3. The loving church had become more of a church of duty and Jesus was no longer the central figure in their lives and witness, so they needed to get back to a more intimate relationship with Him through praise, worship, prayer and Bible study.

2 *SMYRNA* (Verses 8-11)   *Era Date: AD 96–313*

   Church Name Meaning: Suffering

   - This church represented the suffering church. It had suffered great persecution but remained faithful to Jesus. He commends their faithfulness.
   - During this era, Christians were persecuted and killed for refusing to worship Caesar as god. Only Jews were exempt.
   - The Judaizers, were a group of so-called Jewish Christians, who promoted a false teaching that the Mosaic Law† should be part of their Christian faith and that Gentile converts to Christianity must first be circumcised. Jesus' death is a gift to Christians through

†See Glossary

God's grace. Nothing else is required. He did it all. By missing this important point, the Judaizers were leading Christians into apostasy†. The Judaizers were, therefore, called the Synagogue of Satan.

- Ignatius of Antioch, was an early Christian writer who knew the apostles John and Paul. He made it clear that Christianity came out of Judaism, not the other way round.

The 10 Days

The 10 days are symbolic of 10 periods of persecution that tried to stop the spread of the Gospel.

1. Domitian (AD 96)
2. Trajan (AD 98–117)
3. Hadrian (AD 117–138)
4. Antonius Pius (AD 138–161)
5. Marcus Aurelis (AD 161-180)
6. Septimus Severus (AD 193–211)
7. Maximin (AD 235–238)
8. Decius (AD 249–251)
9. Valarian (AD 251–260)
10. Diocletian (AD 284–305)

3 PERGAMOS (Verses 12-17)   Era Date: AD 313-800 (in England)
                              AD 313-306 (in some other countries)

Church Name Meaning: Thoroughly married

Pergamos was the capital city of the kingdom of Pergamum. It had a healing spa but was not a commercial city.

The doctrines of Balaam and the Nicolations were erroneous teachings of false grace. They held the view that Christians were free from any form of law and, consequently, could indulge themselves in any way they pleased. Satan was using these doctrines to deceive believers into thinking that sinful practises and worldliness were acceptable to God.

†See Glossary

However, these false teachings totally denied the law of Christ which is written on the hearts of true believers (Hebrews 8:10 and Jeremiah 31:33).

> "This is the new covenant I will make
> with my people on that day, says the Lord:
> I will put my laws in their hearts,
> and I will write them on their minds."

In Romans 6:12-15, Paul writes that Christians should not give in to sinful desires but give themselves completely to God.

- The Balaam doctrine permitted sexual immorality and joining in with the feasts given to venerate pagan idols.
- The Nicolatians (which means one who conquers, dominates and rules) followed the Balaam doctrine to some extent but also advocated that the Church should fit in with the world instead of resisting the world's values and preaching the Gospel. They lusted for power. However, some in the Church did not follow either of these forms of corruption and remained true to God.

The Pergamum Church represents the beginning of Christianity becoming a state religion.

- In AD 312, Constantine issued the Edict of Milan, reversing the persecution of Christians throughout the Empire. Christianity became the government favoured status; i.e. Christianity became "thoroughly married" to the state by becoming the state religion.
- As a result, many pagan influences crept into the Church.
- Non-Biblical customs were adopted, e.g. praying for the dead, praying to saints and to Mary and some commentators think that they wore clerical robes to separate the clergy from the laity. However, certainly now, if not then, many clergy view their robes as the sacred vestments of their office, directing the thoughts of the congregation away from them so that God alone can be glorified in the services they perform for Him. Some also feel an added closeness to God as they don their sacred robes, thus making them better prepared for ministry.

4 **THYATIRA (verses 18-29)**   *Era Date: AD 800–1517 (in England)*
                                   AD 606-1517 (in some other countries)

Church Name Meaning: Continual sacrifice

- There were many individuals in this church who truly loved and served Christ. God commends the church for their love, works and patient service.

- The feet of fine brass speak of the judgement to come.

- The eyes of fire speak of God's omniscience†. It may also denote His anger at seeing all the sin and corruption in the church.

- The Jezebel spirit present in this church led believers to commit sexual immorality and participate in the worship of pagan idol feasts. The Jezebel spirit also represented the teaching of worldliness just like the Balaam doctrine. However, the Jezebel spirit led to a higher level of apostasy†.

The Thyatira Church represents the Era of the Medieval Roman Catholic Church institution. The Roman Catholic Church began about 606 AD when Bishop Boniface III was given the title of 'Pope' meaning bishop over all bishops and thus universal bishop of Rome.

- This Church was 'married' to the state. It used its powers to launch the Crusades and Inquisitions.

- The Church now adopted customs not found in the Bible, like confession to a priest who absolved them from their sin. The people were gradually weaned away from trusting Christ alone as their Saviour and Mediator before God, towards man-made rules and regulations, which put the Church in authority over the people. Salvation was taught as being earned through works rather than purely by faith.

- The Church was able to control the people who could only receive whatever sermons they were given. Many were unable to check for themselves the accuracy of the 'truths' they were being told because they were unable to read the Bible or did not possess one.
- The Church claimed exclusive authority over the interpretation of God's Word so believers were not allowed to disagree.

    Notable reformers in this era:
    John Wycliffe (1330-1384) is well known for being the first person to translate the Bible into English. Because he was a reformer, he attacked the beliefs and practises of the Church of his day.
    John Huss (1370-1415) was also known as Jan Hus. He was influenced by John Wycliffe and became the most important Czech reformer of the 15th century. He was burned at the stake in 1415.

Commentary on Chapter 3

5 SARDIS (verses 1-6)   *Era Date: AD 1517–1660*

Church Name Meaning: Those escaping

Sardis was an active, wealthy, commercial city. Originally, it was situated on a small, elevated plateau that rose steeply above the Hermus Valley, the only access being by a steep and difficult path on the south side. The other sides were almost smooth and sheer.

Later, the city was extended to incorporate another, larger, site in the valley. The plain on which the lower part of the city was situated was well watered and a thriving carpet industry was established there, which brought the people much wealth.

They thought that they had all they needed financially and also thought they were secure from attack owing to their geographical location, which caused them to become lax and apathetic. 'Impenetrable' Sardis was captured twice because of their apathy towards guarding the city. The first time was by Cyrus of Persia in 549 BC, while the second was by Antiochus in 218 BC.

The Church at Sardis is condemned most severely – a city that began with a good reputation is in fact dead, owing to their spiritual apathy.

The Church is told to be watchful and to avoid lacking spiritual vigilance or they will find that Christ will come unexpectedly and some will miss Him.

Those in the Sardis Church who have remained loyal and true to the Lord will have their names read out in heaven to the Father and the angels. These people, Jesus tells them, belong to Him.

- The Sardis Church represents the Era of the Reformation, leading to the formation of the Protestant Church.
- The Reformation began when, in 1517, Martin Luther posted his 95 objections to the Roman Catholic faith.
- The fundamental principle of the Reformation was to restore the Bible as the sole and final authority for Christian faith and practice, rather than the teachings and traditions of the Church.

6 PHILADELPHIA (verses 7-13)   *Era Date: AD 1660–the Rapture*

Church Name Meaning: Brotherly love

The Church at Philadelphia represents the revived Protestant Church.

In the two Church Eras that followed the Sardis Era, the Church that **learns from** Christ's commands to the Sardis Church becomes the Church at Philadelphia.

- It is a missionary city, built as a centre of Greek civilisation.
- It is positioned at the centre of several important trade routes and is called 'The Gateway to the East'. Therefore, the Church is able to reach the whole region.

Its beliefs are based on New Testament teachings:
- Justification by faith in Christ alone for salvation.
- Biblical principles direct life.

- A personal relationship with Jesus brings joy, which overflows into witnessing.
- It became the Evangelical branch of the Church.

7 *LAODICEA* (verses 14-22)   *Era Date:*   *AD 1890 onward*

   Church Name Meaning: People ruling

The Church that **does not learn from** Christ's commands to the Church at Sardis becomes the Laodicean Church.

Jesus' reprimand that they are a lukewarm church would have resonated with the Laodiceans owing to their water problem. Drinking water was scarce and had to be piped in, via an aqueduct, from a hot spring in Hieropolis (see Map 1), north of Laodicea. However, by the time the hot water reached Laodicea, it had become tepid.

Laodicea was a wealthy community, having made their wealth from:

1. The wool trade — garments they made from the glossy black wool from the sheep they bred were much sought after.
2. Eye salve — made from the boracic acid found in that area.

They had nothing to commend them. Because they were self sufficient and not dependent on God, they were spiritually wretched, miserable and blind.

Laodicea represents the apostate† Church Era.

- A church that rejects the authority of God's Word, using secular thought to shape the church, not vice versa.
- A church ruled by men, for men.
- Christ is on the outside and the Holy Spirit is not present.

The roots of Protestant Liberalism begin to become apparent in:
- The rise of humanism and secular thought.
- The rise of anti-Biblical philosophy, e.g. Darwin's Theory of Evolution (1859).
- Adopting the higher criticism of German commentators in the late 1800s, which attacked the Divine origin, authority, inerrancy† and accuracy of the Bible.

N.B. Liberal theology rejects the Bible as the inerrant† Word of God. Jesus longs for members of this church to return to Him as He knocks on the door of their hearts.

The Rapture

The Rapture is the name given to the sudden return of Christ in the clouds to snatch up all Christians from the earth. *This is not the Second Coming.*

1 Thessalonians 4:15-18 tells us the order in which Christians will be raptured:

1. The bodies of those who have died in Christ and whose spirits are in heaven will rise first.
2. The bodies and spirits of those who are Christians living at this time will then be caught up in the clouds with Jesus.

The Rapture will happen:

- suddenly and unexpectedly, as a thief in the night (1 Thessalonians 5:2).
- at a time when life is going on as usual (as in the days of Noah and Lot, before God's judgement came – Luke 17:26)
- before Christ returns to earth in glory.

The timing of this event is unknown. Some people believe that Christians will go through (all or part of) the Tribulation. However,

1. The Old Testament prophecies in such books as Isaiah, Daniel and Ezekiel relate to the events John saw in his Revelation, which are solely pertinent to the Jewish nation; also
2. The Church is not mentioned on earth after chapter 3 until Revelation chapter 19:7-8, where she is referred to as the 'bride of Christ'†. The Elders in chapter 4 represent the Church. Many commentators deem it most likely that the Rapture will happen before the Tribulation. I am, therefore, following this interpretation. This means that the Rapture could happen at any time between now and the Tribulation, covered in chapters 6 to 19.

The Book of Revelation
Chapter 4
The Church in Heaven

Revelation moves to a time after the Rapture of the Church.

These things will take place in the future.

Commentary on chapter 4

Verses 1-2   John hears the voice of God sounding like a trumpet. He sees an open door and God invites him to "come up here." John does this and finds himself in the throne room of God.

Some commentators see John as a 'type'† of the church. Thus, the raptured church is now in the throne room of heaven.

The only other people to be invited to "come up here" are the two witnesses (Moses and Elijah – see page 24), after they rise from the dead (Revelation 11:12).

The One on the throne

Verse 3   There are two main schools of thought as to the identity of the One on the throne:

1. He is both the Father and the Son.

   The Father and the Son are One (based on verses such as John 10:30,38 and 17:5). Some think that, if we faced the light of the Father's holiness on His throne, we would be facing a Throne of Judgement. However, as Jesus has intervened on our behalf through His saving sacrifice on the cross, He has brought about our reconciliation with God and, therefore, it is for us the Throne of Grace, not the Throne of Judgement.

2. The Father alone is on the throne.
   Many commentators suggest that these gemstones represent just the Father because the slain Lamb of God appears in chapters 5 and 6.

In interpretation 1:

JASPER The Jasper stone represents the Father. Jasper stones can range in colour from browns, reds, yellows and blues to whites, the most common being red. The exact colour of the stone here is not mentioned.

SARDIUS The Sardius stone represents Jesus. It is a blood red stone.

Of note is the fact that Jasper and Sardius were the first and last stones on the Jewish High Priest's breast plate. They are also found in the walls of the New Jerusalem (Revelation 21:18-19).

EMERALD BOW symbolises the multifaceted life and grace of God, radiating out of the throne in the form of the Holy Spirit, flowing from the Father through the Son.

In interpretation 2: The two stones represent the Father.
The emerald bow represents the Holy Spirit.

In both interpretations:

The colour green represents life.

ELDERS: Represent the whole Church. Their bowls
Verse 4 contain incense, i.e. the prayers of God's people. (Compare Revelation 5:8-10.)
Interestingly, King David organised his priests into 24 divisions, each with its own High Priest (1 Chronicles 24:1-19).

Verse 5 The 7 torches represent the sevenfold Holy Spirit.

4 LIVING CREATURES Verses 6-8	They are seraphim or cherubim, i.e. angelic beings. Compare Ezekiel Ch.1:5-10 where each cherubim had 4 faces. The faces symbolise 4 aspects of God's nature that flow out of His presence and throne. But, in Revelation, John sees each cherubim having only one type of face but each differing from the faces of the other three.
	The Eyes indicate that they are alert and aware.
LION:	symbolises ruling power, dominion and authority.
MAN:	symbolises love.
EAGLE:	symbolises understanding and wisdom.
OX:	symbolises power for service.
Verses 9-11	The role of the living beings is to worship God. As they worship and give honour and glory to God, the 24 elders also worship God.

As we open our souls and spirits to God to enable Him to work in and through us, the Holy Spirit will empower us to be like:

The LION when we need to exercise authority.

The MAN when we are relating to people.

The EAGLE when we need to discern wisdom and truth.

The OX when we have to bear a heavy burden or need to focus on a task God has given us to do.

The Book of Revelation
Chapter 5
Jesus alone has the legal right to open the Scroll

Background

Legal land purchase agreements in Old Testament times

To understand the document with the seals in chapter 5 and the problem of finding someone worthy to open them, we need to go back to the Jewish Law in these matters.

Jewish Law of Redemption

1. All land belongs to God. He owns the Title Deeds.

2. The Promised Land was given to Israel as an inheritance (see Map 2). Each of the 12 tribes of Israel was allocated a portion of the land and each family within the tribe, a portion of that portion as tenant-possessors (see Map 3).

3. The tribes of Israel were Tenant-Possessors and, as such, could not sell or hand over the land as a permanent contract.

4. If control of the Title Deeds of all or part of a person's land had to be sold because they had fallen on hard times, it had to be returned to the original owner in the Year of Jubilee, which happened every 49 years.

5. If one family got into debt and needed to sell their rights to a parcel of land, a kinsman (i.e. a relative) could buy it from them and, in so doing, save their relative from hardship or prison. The kinsman here was called a 'kinsman redeemer'. (We see this demonstrated in the Book of Ruth, when Boaz acts as kinsman redeemer and redeems the land for Ruth's mother-in-law.)

The Law stated that, in the Year of Jubilee any purchased land must be returned to the original tenant-possessor. That person was then back in his original rightful place through God's grace in giving the year of Jubilee.

Map 2 shows the extent of the land covenanted by God to Abraham[1] (circa 2065 B.C.), Isaac[2], Jacob[3] and their descendants[4]

[1]Abraham: Genesis 15:18-20
[2]Isaac: Genesis 26:2-6
[3]Jacob: Genesis 28:13-15
[4]Descendants: Genesis 15:18-21

Map 3: shows an approximate distribution of the land occupied by the 12 tribes of Israel (Joshua chapters 13-19)

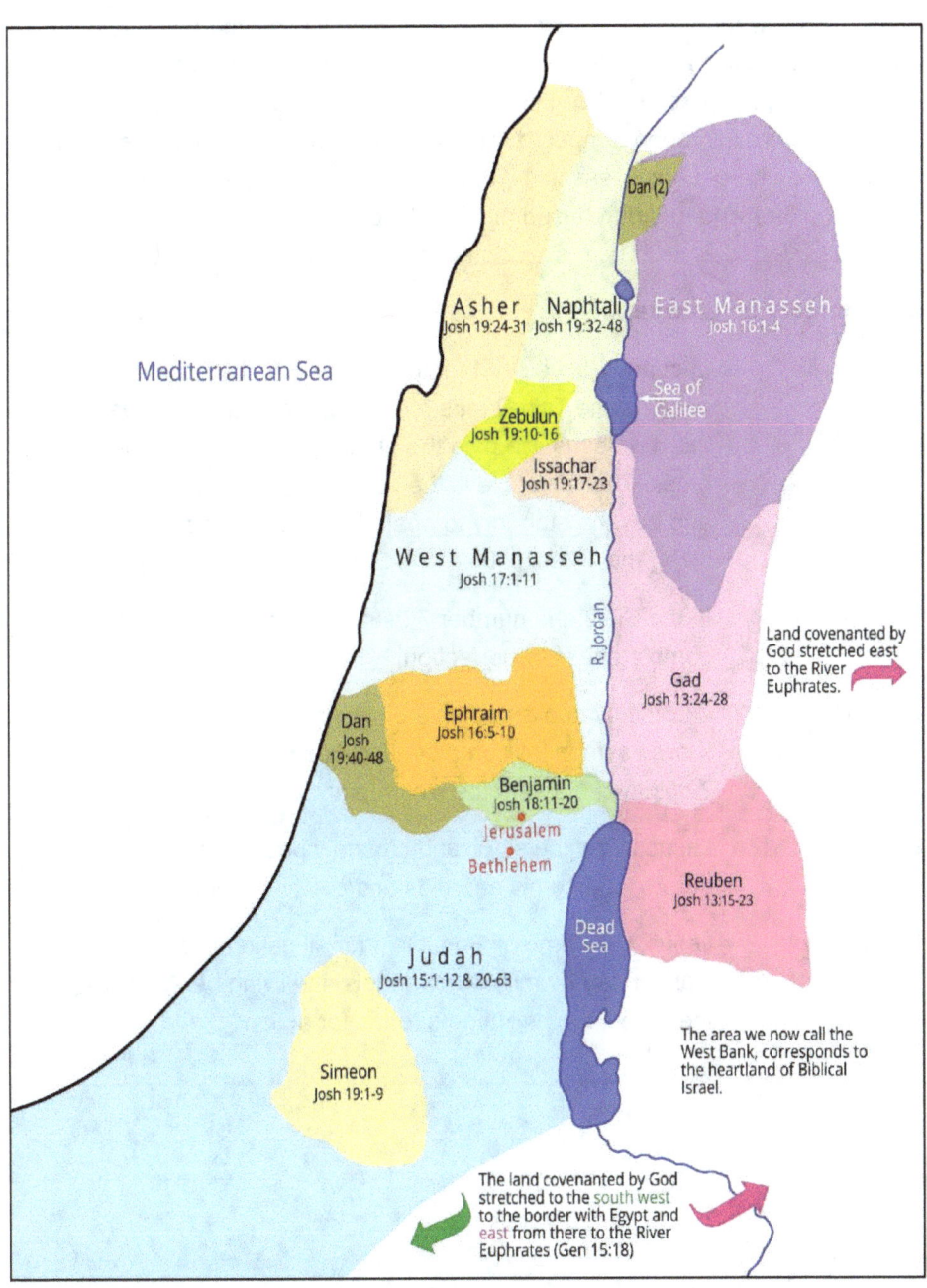

Legal Land Purchase agreements in Old Testament times

When a legal document was drawn up, two copies were made. One was given to the owner of the Title Deeds and the other was sealed and put in a safe place – such as a clay pot (Jeremiah 32:10-14). If there was any dispute about the purchaser's rights or if it was felt that his copy of the legal document had been tampered with, the sealed copy was produced and opened, in front of witnesses, by the person with the legal right to do so, i.e. the one who had purchased the Title Deeds.

Commentary on Chapter 5

Verses 1-5	In chapter 5 we see that the person who has paid the price for the Title Deeds of the Earth and all who dwell there is Jesus. He paid the price by His death on the cross. Therefore, He is the only One Who is worthy and has the authority to open the scroll, the scroll being the Title Deeds of the Earth.
	In the Bible, the number 7 usually represents completeness or perfection.
Verse 6	7 horns symbolise complete power. 7 eyes symbolise complete knowledge. 7 spirits of God are the Holy Spirit.
Verse 7	Jesus takes the scroll and can now possess the earth before judging his enemies and evicting them from it.
Verses 8-14	Jesus, the Lamb of God, slain for all nations, is worshipped by millions of angels, the living beings and the 24 elders, as He gets ready for action.

N.B. Jesus is now standing ready for action. He is our kinsman redeemer and is ready to redeem both mankind and the whole earth and to punish and judge once and for all, all the evil and the evil powers in His world. Satan will no longer be the 'Prince (or Ruler) of this World' (John 16:11) but will be overcome and locked up for 1,000 years (as we shall see later in the book), until he is finally destroyed at the end of this time by being thrown into the fiery lake of burning sulfur (Revelation 20:10).

Overview of the Tribulation

1. The Rapture of the Church of Jesus Christ is before the day the Tribulation begins and the first six seals are opened.

2. After that, there is an unspecified period of time while the Antichrist becomes close in his relations with Israel.

3. When the 7th seal is opened, in chapter 7, the Antichrist has made a covenant with the Jewish Nation. The 2 witnesses and the 144,000 Messianic Jews† begin their ministries.

4. The Tribulation lasts for 7 years.

   A   The first 3½ years are the years before the Antichrist shows his true colours to Israel and he allows the Jews to make sacrifices to God in the newly built third Temple. The two witnesses, Moses and Elijah (representing the Law and the Prophets), witness on the Temple Mount to the fact that Jesus Christ is the Messiah. The 144,000 Messianic Jews† travel far and wide in an evangelistic campaign.

   The judgements of the 6 trumpets are complete. The 7th trumpet, containing the 7 bowls, continues to the end.

   B   After a short interlude (maybe weeks or a few months) the Jews in Israel who have become Christians as a result of the preaching of the 2 witnesses and the 144,000 evangelists flee to the wilderness where they remain until Jesus rescues them at His second coming.

   C   At the beginning of the second 3½ years, the Antichrist reneges on the treaty and desecrates the temple with a large image of himself. Daniel 12:11 speaks of this:

   > From the time the daily sacrifice is stopped and the sacrilegious object that causes desecration is set up to be worshipped, there will be 1,290 days.

   There is much suffering during this 3½ years until the whole Jewish nation finally repents and accepts Jesus as their Messiah.

The Tribulation ends at the Battle of Armageddon with Jesus' return in power to rescue the remaining Jews, who are being held under siege. He then deals with all the evil powers in the world in readiness for His millennial reign on earth.

For Jesus' comments on the Tribulation and the End Times, please see the notes on Matthew chapter 24, Jesus' Olivet Discourse, which is Appendix 1.

For more details of Daniel's prophecies that relate to the Tribulation, see Appendix 2.

The Judgements

A short explanation about the following judgements might be helpful.

Firstly, it should be said that these judgements are designed to shake up the unbelievers on earth and, indeed, during this time many of them will come to know the Lord.

There are three sets of Judgements:

1. Seals
2. Trumpets
3. Bowls

There are 7 of each type of judgement and the 7th of each holds the judgements of the next set.

i.e. **Seal 7**

Contains all the judgements of the 7 trumpets.

Trumpet 7

Contains all the judgements of the 7 bowls.

Each new set of judgements grows in intensity, with the bowls being the last and greatest judgements.

When the last judgement of the 7th bowl is complete there are no more judgements.

The Book of Revelation
Chapter 6
Judgements of the Seals

This chapter marks the beginning of the Tribulation.

Commentary on chapter 6

The first 6 seals are opened, one after the other in quick succession.

Each time a seal is broken, Jesus is bringing devastation to a different realm of the world order.

In this chapter, God begins to withdraw His protection, mercy and grace, from the world.

Seal 1 White horse Verse 2		Judgement of the political realm. The rider on the white horse, the Antichrist, is released to begin his attempt to conquer the world. He appears to be peaceful but he is not.
Seal 2 Red horse Verse 4		Judgement of the international realm. Red denotes terror and blood-shed. God removes His peace from the earth therefore there are more wars.
Seal 3 Black horse Verse 5		Judgement of the financial realm. God's withdrawal leads to hyperinflation and chaos resulting in hunger and misery, famine and more deaths.
Seal 4 Pale horse Verse 8		God withdraws His hand of protection over life. Disease, famine and wars will increase. A quarter of the earth will die.
Seal 5 Verse 9		John sees, in heaven, the souls of those who have been martyred for their faith. They are praying that God will avenge their blood. Each of them is then clothed in a white

	Moral realm	garment and told to rest until all the remaining souls to be martyred have joined them. Some commentators believe that this is the point at which God withdraws His moral restraint, leading to martyrdom, abuse, pain, fear and horror.
Seal 6 Verse 12	Nature	God withdraws from the natural world. Devastation of the natural world and cosmic changes ensue, including:

- earthquakes
- volcanic explosions
- tsunamis
- meteor showers
- asteroids colliding with the earth

People are frightened by these judgements, wanting to hide themselves and they wonder who would be able to survive God's wrath. (Logically, does this not indicate that they knew they had rebelled against God?)

The Book of Revelation
Chapter 7
The Interlude and beyond

Background

This chapter begins to hone in on the Jewish nation.

At this time, if not a little before, the Antichrist makes a peace treaty with Israel for 7 years. During this time, he allows a third Temple to be built on the Temple Mount. He also allows sin offerings to be made there to Yahweh.

> The ruler will make a treaty with the people for a period of one set of seven, but after half this time, he will put an end to the sacrifices and offerings. (Daniel 9:27a)
> (1 set of 7 is 7 years – Appendix 2, page 93)

At the same time, the 2 witnesses, Moses and Elijah, begin their ministry on the Temple Mount (Revelation 11:4-12). The Jews will understand that Moses represents the Law and Elijah the prophets. These witnesses will be able to reveal Jesus to the Jews as the Jewish Messiah, using prophesies from the Old Testament which relate to Jesus (Revelation 11:3).

After 3½ years the Antichrist reneges on his promised peace treaty, stops the sacrifices and has a large statue representing himself placed in the temple, thus defiling God's holy place.

> And as a climax to all his terrible deeds, he will set up a sacrilegious object that causes desecration, until the fate decreed for this defiler is finally poured out on him. (Daniel 9 27b)

Commentary on Chapter 7

There is a delay, probably of a few months, between the opening of the sixth and seventh seals. Chapter 7 records what happens during this interlude.

The opening of the 7th seal will unleash all the judgements of the 7 trumpets, which will be more severe than the seals.

Verses 1-3   The angels in verses 1-3 are the angels who will blow the first 4 trumpets. They are held back for a very important reason:

12,000 Jews from each of the 12 tribes of Israel need to be 'sealed', i.e. they need to receive a seal of God's protection.

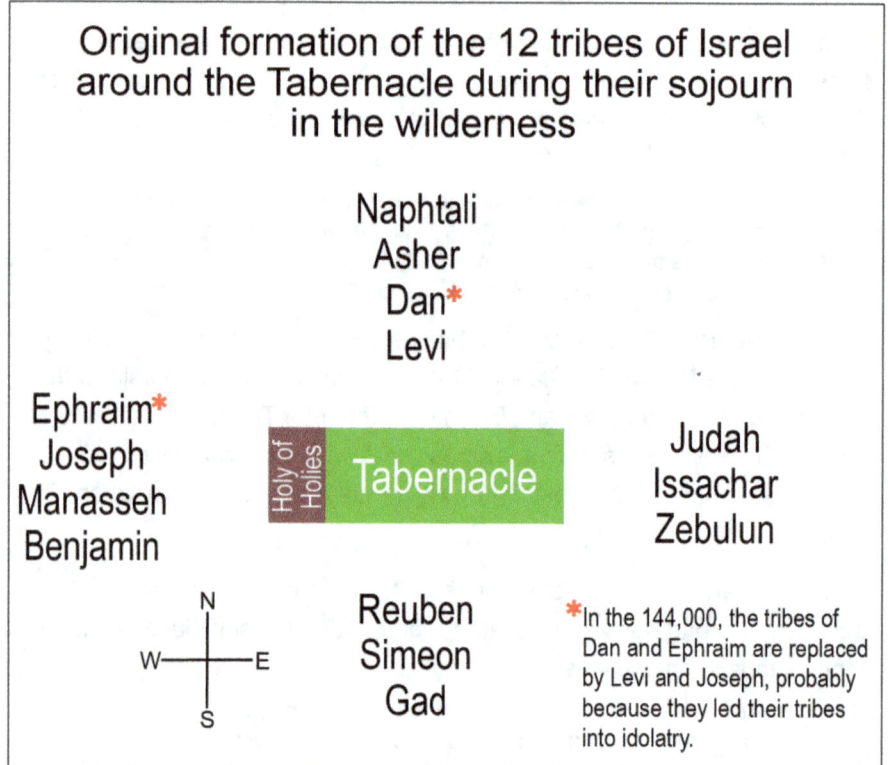

Verses 4-8   These 144,000 Jews begin a world-wide evangelistic crusade. So we see that God is unwavering in His desire to save as many souls as possible. Many people will have begun to question what they believe after the first 6 seals and so will be more open to receiving the gospel.

Verses 9-17   John now sees ahead to the results of the worldwide evangelistic crusade by the 144,000 and the 2 witnesses (Moses and Elijah). Innumerable people from all nations are in heaven at the end of the Tribulation. They are dressed in white and hold palms, which denote triumph. They are declaring that salvation comes from the Father and the Son. There is great rejoicing in heaven because of the salvation of these souls and the victory that has been won through Jesus.

These people from every nation have not taken the mark of the beast† (Revelation 13:16-17) owing to their faith in Christ. Many will have been martyred for their faith and we see them here, back where they belong, worshipping God and the Lamb. Jesus, their shepherd, will protect and love them tenderly for evermore.

The Book of Revelation
Chapter 8
Judgements of Trumpets 1-4

Author's note

It is difficult for us to understand why God will allow the suffering during the Tribulation. I believe that it is important for us to remember:

- God is holy, righteous and merciful. Without His intervention we would all be living in a very dark and broken world.

- Mankind needs to experience what life in a world devoid of God's grace is like: they can then make an informed choice either for Him or against Him.

- The length of the Tribulation is 7 years in total. The last 3½ years are the worst.

- The suffering of those who will exist for eternity without God's love and protection will be worse than we could ever imagine.

- God needs to use the suffering of the Tribulation to get people's attention. If there were a better way, God in His righteousness would do it. (He has already demonstrated this by allowing His Son to die on the cross to purchase our salvation.)

    "For this is how God loved the world: He gave His one and only Son, so that everyone who believes in Him will not perish but have eternal life. (John 3:16)

    "...He is being patient for your sake. He does not want anyone to be destroyed, but wants everyone to repent." (2 Peter 3:9)

Commentary on chapter 8

Seal 7
Verse 1

God asserts His Lordship over all heavenly and demonic realms.

The silence, when Jesus opens the 7th seal, underlines the seriousness of the judgements of God to come. The 7th seal contains all the judgements of the trumpets, which follow.

Verse 2

The 7 angels are given the 7 trumpets.

Verses 3-4

The picture of the angel with the golden incense burner that is full of incense mixed with the prayers of God's people, assures us that all our prayers have been kept for this important time. As the prayers of God's people have risen up, so judgement is about to come down to satisfy God's righteousness and avenge the wrongs and injustices suffered by His children throughout history.

The prayers of the saints offered under the 5th seal (Rev. 6:10) are now being answered because of all that Jesus accomplished on the cross.

N.B. The 144,000 Messianic Jews† who have been sealed will be protected from the judgements to come.

Verse 5

The angel takes the incense burner and throws it to earth.

Verse 6

The 7 angels begin to sound the 7 trumpets.

Trumpet 1
Verse 7

Destroys one third of all plant life and all the grass. Therefore, there will be ecological ramifications.

Trumpet 2
Verses 8-9

Something which looks akin to a very large, fiery mountain is thrown into the sea, making a third of it blood red. Therefore, one third of all life in the sea and a third of all ships on the sea are destroyed. Up to half of the oxygen we use is produced by oceanic plankton. Therefore, the planet's oxygen will be much depleted.

Trumpet 3
Verses 10-11

A great burning star falls on a third of the rivers. Therefore, one third of all life in fresh water is destroyed. With drinking water compromised in some parts of the world, many will die.

Trumpet 4
Verses 12-13

One third of all natural light sources darken (i.e. sun, moon and stars). This will affect the growth of crops and all plant life.

These first 4 trumpet judgements adversely affect the earth's ecosystems. The last three trumpets are worse because they are described as 'woes' and will bring intensity of judgement to people on earth.

The Counterfeit, Satanic Trinity

Satan often counterfeits the holy things of God.

Yahweh, the God of the Bible, is a holy trinity:
>Father – the Head
>Son – Jesus, our Saviour
>Holy Spirit – Who, for example, empowers
>>Christians and leads them into all truth

Satan has created a false, counterfeit trinity:
>Satan – the Head
>Antichrist
>False Prophet

Satan

He is the counterfeit of the Father.

We have already met him in chapter 5. He is the prince of this world but he will only remain active until King Jesus comes to reign. Satan directs the work of the Antichrist and the false prophet.

Antichrist

He is the counterfeit, i.e. opposite, of Jesus.

He is a man who comes onto the world stage before the beginning of the Tribulation. He is controlled, empowered and directed by Satan in his deception and cruel persecution of Jews and Christians. He offers peace and is greatly admired by world leaders. He becomes the most important world leader. He makes a peace treaty with Israel but reneges on it after 3½ years.

He is sometimes referred to as *The Beast who comes out of the Sea*.

He dies but rises from the dead.

He is assisted in his work by the false prophet.

False Prophet

He is the counterfeit of the Holy Spirit.

He encourages people to worship the Antichrist in the second half of the Tribulation.

The Book of Revelation
Chapter 9
Judgements of Trumpets 5 and 6 (Woes 1 and 2)

Introduction

The 3 woes denote escalating severity of judgement. God has removed His grace from the earth and allowed those rebelling against Him to be subject to the powers of darkness.

We meet the following characters in this chapter and they are all titles of Satan or demonic beings.

- The Destroyer, Abaddon   S
- star   S
- locusts   D
- scorpions   D
- cavalry   D

Key:
S = Satan
D = demonic beings

Demons are fallen angels, who were once in heaven. They rebelled against God, left heaven and became the power of evil in the world, ruled over by their leader, Satan, who is the most powerful fallen angel.

The star that has fallen from the sky is Satan.

He is given the key to the bottomless pit, which contains the worst of the demons. Even demons were afraid of those in the bottomless pit!

> [30] Jesus demanded, "What is your name?"
>
> "Legion," he replied, for he was filled with many demons. [31] The demons kept begging Jesus not to send them into the bottomless pit. (Luke 8:30-31)

Trumpet 5 tells us of demonic attacks. The powers of the demons in Trumpet 5 are limited, their purpose being to torment people for 5 months.

Commentary on chapter 9

Trumpet 5   The first woe brings the first terror.

1ˢᵗ WOE   John sees a terrifying sight.

Verses 1-12   The fallen angel (called The Destroyer or Satan) is allowed to open the bottomless pit.

Very thick, dark smoke pours out of the bottomless pit.

Demons appear out of the thick smoke that blots out the sun. They emerge as an army prepared for battle. They look like locusts but have tails like scorpions. As rows and rows of them come into view in the sky, it appears as if they are a formation of horses wearing iron armour and their wings make a terrifying roaring sound. On their heads are crowns, which denote power. Their heads are unusual in that they have human faces and hair – which might make them appear approachable. However, they have lions' teeth!

The main source of torment seems to be from the scorpion's tail, whose sting causes horrendous pain.

The scorpion demons are given their power for 5 months. Their king is The Destroyer, Satan, who is also known as Abaddon.

The demons have rankings under their king, Satan.

N.B. These demons will not damage any plant life. Also, people who bear the seal of Jesus will not be harmed. These Christians will have come to accept Jesus as their Saviour after the Rapture because of the teaching of the 2 witnesses and the 144,000 Jews we heard about in chapter 7.

Trumpet 6

2ⁿᵈ WOE
Verses 13-21

The sixth trumpet brings the second terror.

One third of the human population will be killed. The four fallen angels (i.e. Satan's angels), who have been bound up until this point, are released and instigate the invasion by the cavalry.

N.B. These angels are fallen angels held at the River Euphrates until this time, not the four holy angels we met in chapter 7.

The cavalry is also demonic.

These demons invade the earth in their droves. We are told that the army is 200 million demons strong.

The invading demons are seen as horses, each with a breast plate of fiery red, hyacinth blue and pale yellow. The heads of the horses are lions and the plagues of fire, smoke and brimstone stream from their mouths.

Theses plagues kill one third of the human population remaining on earth. The picture is similar to the destruction of Sodom and Gomorrah (Genesis 19:1-29) but it will be much more widespread, severe, intense and devastating.

As well as the plagues, the horse demons can kill with their lion mouths and serpent tails.

The one notable difference between the two armies in this chapter is that the locusts only harm mankind whereas the cavalry kills them.

The whole point of this escalation in judgement is so that the remainder of mankind will see the error of their ways and turn to God, thus avoiding the even greater continuing pain, horror and torment of eternity in hell without God, who has hitherto been their protector.

The end of the period of the 6th trumpet marks mid-Tribulation. At this time, the 2 witnesses have just been martyred, have risen again after 3 days and gone to heaven. (More details are given in chapter 11.)

The Book of Revelation
Chapter 10
An interlude (which continues into chapters 11 &12)

Background

By this point, approximately half of the world's population will have left the earth, either because of the rapture or through death as a result of the judgements of the seals and trumpets.

On the time scale of the 7 year Tribulation, we have reached the midpoint.

Introduction

Chapters 10-12 are a single vision. The pause between the 6th Trumpet and the 7th is the longest interlude recorded in the Book of Revelation. This not only denotes the seriousness of the judgements to come, but also demonstrates God's desire for people to have time to consider what has already happened and realise that their hope lies in Him alone.

Commentary on Chapter 10

Verses 1-3   The identity of the mighty angel is not certain but the two main schools of thought are:

1. He is just another mighty angel (possibly Michael, whose name means *Like God*) with great power and authority conveying a message to John. The reasoning here is that Jesus is referred to as the Lamb in Revelation so it is thought by this group that this is not Jesus.

2. He is Jesus. The reasoning here being that He had one foot on the land and one in the sea (denoting authority over land and sea) and that He roared like a lion (the Lion of Judah?).

Verses 4-6	When the angel shouted, he was replied to by 7 thunders. The term '7 thunders' is used in the Old Testament to portray the voice of God (e.g. Psalm 29:3 and Job 37:5).
	John, who is ready to write down what God is saying, is told not to do so because it is a secret.
Verse 7	We are then told that, when the 7th angel blows his trumpet, God's mysterious plan will be fulfilled as the prophets foretold.
This tells us:	

- that the 7th trumpet goes on blowing until Christ's return.
- when Christ returns to earth, all the prophecies in the Bible will have to come to pass and the mystery will have been revealed.

Many commentators believe that the secret mystery is the Church Age (see chapters 2 and 3).

Verses 8-10	As John eats the little book (the Word of God), it is both sweet to the taste (because of the ultimate victory of Jesus) and bitter in the stomach (because of the judgements of God yet to come before the final victory).

The Word of God is full of God's love and grace and truth so it is sweet and, having absorbed God's Word, John is again in a position to prophecy to the nations about the things that are to come as God reveals them to him.

In stark contrast is the bitterness of the judgement of Satan, the demons and the human wrongs of non- believers, who will be severely judged and punished because they have rejected God's gift of salvation.

Verse 11 John is now told to prophesy.

The Book of Revelation
Chapter 11
The 2 Witnesses and the 3rd Woe

Commentary on chapter 11

Verses 1-3   Leading up to the Tribulation, a world ruler will emerge who signs a treaty with Israel. In the treaty, the leader (who appears to be a peacemaker but is, in fact, the Antichrist) agrees to allow a 3rd Temple to be built on the Temple Mount. In the opening verses, John sees the new Temple being measured up.

The outer courtyard of the Temple is not measured as Muslims will still have the administrative rights to this land. At this point in time they will, therefore, have free reign to move about on it.

The purpose of this third Temple is to remind Jews of their former understanding: that sins are forgiven when blood sacrifices of animals are made to God. This renewed practise will, therefore, help them to understand Jesus' sacrifice and the shedding of His blood on the cross, in their place, for their sin.

Verses 4-6   John reflects back to look in more detail at the ministry of the 2 witnesses. There is reference to them in Zechariah's prophecy (chapter 4:2, 3, 11 and 14):

> [2] "What do you see now?" he asked.
>
> I answered, "I see a solid gold lampstand with a bowl of oil on top of it. Around the bowl are seven lamps, each having seven spouts with wicks. [3] And I see two olive trees, one on each side of the bowl."
>
> [11] Then I asked the angel, "What are these two olive trees on each side of the lampstand?"
>
> [14] Then he said to me, "They represent the two anointed ones who stand in the court of the Lord of all the earth."

These 2 prophets are Moses and Elijah, also called 'the 2 witnesses'. They are given great power during the first half (3½ years) of the Tribulation while the 3rd Temple is functioning as the House of God. They minister on the Temple Mount to all the world. They are an important part of the Temple ministry, standing against the powers of darkness. If anyone comes near them to do them harm they are killed. The two prophets are also given powers to bring drought (cf. Elijah with King Ahab – 1 Kings 17:1 and 18:44-45) and plagues similar to those in Egypt when Moses went to Pharaoh to ask him to release the Israelites, but, at first, Pharaoh would not let them go. (See especially Exodus 7:14-18 where the River Nile turns to blood.)

Verses 7-10   After the time of their ministry is completed (3½ years) the beast who comes from the bottomless pit (the Antichrist) will kill them and leave their bodies in the main street of Jerusalem. No one buries them. Everyone who does not belong to God is delighted that the Witnesses' reign of plague and drought infliction has come to an end! So much so that they send each other gifts to celebrate!

Verses 11-14   However, after 3½ days, God raises the 2 witnesses from the dead and terror strikes those who see them rise to their feet. Finally, on hearing God's call, the people see them go up to heaven on a cloud. In Jerusalem, a great earthquake demolishes a tenth of the city and 7,000 people die in the earthquake but the people remaining turn to God and give Him glory.

Trumpet 7
3rd WOE
Verses 15-18 — We are now commencing the last half of the Tribulation with the sounding of the 7th Trumpet. The response in heaven is that of great rejoicing because, at last, it is time for Jesus to begin to execute judgement on all the evil in the world. However, no matter how horrendous the imagery becomes in later chapters, we know that it is part of God's plan to flush out the evil so that He can judge every last vestige of it.

Jesus is hailed by the 24 elders to be King over the world. It is His right, therefore, to judge it.

Verse 19 — This verse gives us a glimpse of what is to come in Revelation 15:5 and 8.

The Book of Revelation
Chapter 12
The Woman, the Son and the Dragon

Introduction

Chapter 12 is in the time frame between the Trumpet Judgements and the Bowl Judgements. In this chapter, John gives us an explanation of God's plan of redemption throughout history. Satan is thrown out of heaven and wages war against God by trying to prevent God's plan from happening.

Satan means *adversary* or *enemy*. He is also called in this chapter as:

- the serpent of old (cf. Genesis 3:1)
- the devil (verse 9)
- the deceiver (verse 9)
- the accuser of the brethren (verse 10).

Commentary on Chapter 12

The Woman
verses 1-2

The woman represents Israel. She is associated with the sun, moon and stars as seen in Joseph's dream (Genesis 37:9-10). Jacob is the sun, Rachel, his wife, is the moon and the 12 tribes of Israel are the stars. The Woman is a nation, Israel, not an individual woman. God raised up the Jewish nation through Abraham, Isaac and Jacob.

Fiery red Dragon
Verses 3-4

This is Satan, who took with him a third of the angels of heaven when he rebelled against God. The fallen angels are represented by stars.

The 10 horns denote his power.

The crowns show a status of royalty, i.e. he is a powerful adversary.

Satan uses two approaches to wage war:

1. He opposes what God wants
2. He deceives people.

The Son Verse 5	This is Jesus, the Messiah, Who came into the world through the Jewish nation, Israel. Satan tried to remove Jesus at birth. Herod was his instrument. The latter decreed that all baby boys under the age of 2 should be killed. However, Jesus escaped (Matthew 2:14-18).
	The word for *rule*, here, is better translated as *shepherd.* The iron rod speaks of firmness, not tyranny. With firmness He will, eventually, rid the world of all evil. (Some commentators think that the iron rod is a kingly sceptre.)
	Jesus was rescued from the dragon (Satan) and went to heaven following His crucifixion, resurrection and ascension, where He was given His throne.
Verse 6	This is the moment when the 7th Trumpet is blown. The woman (Israelis who wish to do so, probably mostly Messianic Jews†) flees to the wilderness (verse 14) where she will be protected and provided for, for 1,260 days, which is the second half of the 7 year Tribulation under the Antichrist's dictatorship.
	There is now a pause to allow time for those escaping to reach their place of safety in the wilderness. The wings (verse 14) symbolise the need to flee. In Matthew 24:16-22 Jesus said:

> [16] "Then those in Judea must flee to the hills. [17] A person out on the deck of a roof must not go down into the house to pack. [18] A person out in the field must not return even to get a coat. [19] How terrible it will be for pregnant women and for nursing mothers in those days. [20] And pray that your flight will not be in winter or on the Sabbath. [21] For there will be greater anguish than at any time since the world began. And it will never be so great again. [22] In fact, unless that time of calamity is shortened, not a

	single person will survive. But it will be shortened for the sake of God's chosen ones.
Verse 7	The Archangel Michael stands and is ready for action to protect believing Israel.
	At that time Michael, the archangel who stands guard over your nation, will arise. Then there will be a time of anguish greater than any since nations first came into existence. But at that time every one of your people whose name is written in the book will be rescued. (Daniel 12:1)
Verses 8-11	Satan and his angels are cast down to earth so there is great rejoicing in heaven. Further judgements await Satan and his kingdom, as we shall see when Jesus returns. Satan is no longer able to accuse the brethren (Verse 10).
	Through Jesus' sacrifice on the cross, He saved us from the power of Satan and reconciled us to God. Reference is made to the victory of those who have been martyred because of their faith in Jesus.
	Jesus' power and authority will enable Him to bring God's kingdom on earth into being.
Verses 12-13	The dragon (Satan) is furious and he pursues the woman (Israel), as he knows he has little time left.
Verse 14	Israelis who wish to do so flee to the wilderness, where they will be protected.
Verse 15	The water could be armies of the Antichrist as the word "flood" is often used to represent a large and overwhelming army. The army is swallowed up, probably by an earthquake.
	There is a similarity here with the Children of Israel fleeing from Pharaoh's army but, in that case, it was water that engulfed the enemy army. Some commentators think it might be that the water here is, in fact, a deluge of flood water that is swallowed up in

an earthquake. In either case, the Woman (Israel) is kept safe.

Verse 18 — Satan makes his stand, ready to wage war on God and His people.

Of interest to those who like to see the bigger picture

Satan has always tried to thwart God's plan of redemption, e.g.

- In ancient Egypt, Pharaoh destroyed all the Jewish baby boys, although Moses was rescued (Exodus 1:15-16 and 2:1-10).
- In the Book of Esther, King Xerxes promotes Haman over all the other nobles to become the most powerful official in the Persian empire. Haman hated the Jews. He built a high gallows upon which to hang Mordecai (a Jew who was Queen Esther's guardian) but it was used to hang Haman instead (Esther 7:10).
- Haman's plans for all Jews to be killed was thwarted (Esther 9:1).
- Herod the Great killed all baby boys under 2 years of age but Jesus escaped (Matthew 2:14-18).
- Hitler tried to eradicate the Jews but did not succeed.
- Currently (in 2025), radical Islam is also trying to eradicate the Jews.

Satan never has and never will prevail, as we shall see in the following chapters.

The Book of Revelation
Chapter 13
Opposition to God's Redemptive Plan

Background

The main characters in this chapter are

1. **The Antichrist** – the beast that comes out of the sea.
2. **The False Prophet** - the beast that rises up out of the earth.
3. **Satan** - the dragon.

1. **The Antichrist** is the political world leader.

    Other names for the Antichrist are
    - Man of Lawlessness
    - Son of Perdition (2 Thessalonians 2:3)
    - Worthless Shepherd (Zechariah 11:15-17)
    - The beast that ascends from the bottomless pit (Revelation 11:7)

    We are told in Daniel chapter 11 that the Antichrist will:
    - (verse 36) speak blasphemies against God and continue until the end of the Tribulation
    - (verse 37) have little regard for any gods but
    - (verse 38) he will worship the false god of fortresses
    - (verse 39) he will honour those who submit to him

1. **The False Prophet** is the leader of the world religion instituted by the Antichrist, which viewed the Antichrist as a god who should be worshipped.

2. **Satan** controls both the Antichrist and the false prophet.

Commentary on Chapter 13

Verse 1 — As we have seen, the beast that rises up out of the sea is the Antichrist. He receives his power from Satan.

In the Bible, the sea often represents the Gentile nations. Therefore, the 7 heads are thought to be 7 Gentile powers that have blasphemed against Israel's God (Yahweh).

The 10 horns on the 7th head represent 10 kings, or leaders, who will arise from the last of these kingdoms. They wear crowns, or diadems, because they have great authority.

Verse 2 — The animals here are symbolic of the following empires, as found in Daniel chapter 7 (see Appendix 2, pages 88, 90 and 91, for more details).

Panther (or leopard)	–	Greeco-Macedonian Empire (Daniel 7:6)
Bear	–	Medo-Persia Empire (Daniel 7:5)
Lion	–	Babylonian Empire (Daniel 7:4)

Therefore, the 7th empire will have all the culture of Greece and all the pagan splendour of the Medo-Persian Empire.

It is clear that the 7th head is the empire in power during the Tribulation, initially ruled by 10 kings or leaders. However, the Antichrist eventually takes control of the 7th head and rules with the beast out of the earth (the False Prophet).

The dragon is Satan and he gives his authority and throne to the beast out of the sea.

Verses 3-4	The beast out of the sea (the Antichrist) has been mortally wounded. When the beast recovers from his fatal wound, people worship him.
Verses 5-6	The beast speaks blasphemy against God, for he is given authority to do whatever he wants for 42 months (3½ years, the 2nd half of the Tribulation).
Verses 7-10	The beast is given authority to rule over all nations of the world. He demands homage be paid to him. All who belong to God will not do this so they are persecuted and many are martyred. All of God's people are encouraged to remain faithful.
Verses 11-13	The beast who comes out of the earth is another beast of the same kind, i.e. controlled by Satan. This beast is the false prophet who stages miraculous, counterfeit powers, such as fire flashing down to the earth from the sky (the Satanic equivalent of Elijah calling down holy fire on Mount Carmel – 1 Kings 18:53).
Verses 14-15	This beast, the false prophet, deceives the peoples of the world and detracts attention away from God by the miracles he performs on behalf of the Antichrist. He orders the people to make a statue of the beast of the sea (the Antichrist). He is then allowed to bring the statue to life so that it could speak.
Verses 16-17	All people are required to have the mark of the beast on their person (hand or forehead). Without this mark, they cannot buy or sell anything. Therefore, God's people who are not killed may die from starvation.
Verse 18	The beast's number is 666.

The Book of Revelation
Chapter 14
Harvesting the Nations

Background

We are now commencing the final 3½ years of the Tribulation. This period is often called 'The Great Tribulation'.

The interlude in which Jews and Christians have been able to run to the hills has come to an end. It is time for God to respond to the Antichrist's 'abomination of desolation'†, i.e. his statue in the temple, which is worshipped by those who have not received Jesus as their Saviour (for other references to the 'abomination of desolation' see Daniel 12:11 and Matthew 24:15).

Commentary on chapter 14

Verses 1-5   The chapter opens with a beautiful picture of future events. Jesus is in Jerusalem after His return, with the 144,000. It seems most likely that these are the men who led the evangelistic campaign and were fully protected from the beginning of their ministry when they were sealed by God. These men have kept themselves blameless. Some commentators believe that the 144,000 mentioned here are in heaven with Jesus.

There is great rejoicing in heaven.

The remainder of this chapter gives us a glimpse of what is yet to come, which is expanded upon in chapters 15-19.

There now follows 2 sets of 3 angels (i.e. 6 in all).

Set 1: These angels bring messages

Angel 1   The first angel has an urgency in his message which
Verses 6-7   he delivers to all peoples of the earth. He warns of the judgements to come and urges people to accept Jesus

as their Saviour. It is unique for God to choose an angel to spread the Gospel but, critical here, as his speed of movement will ensure that all of mankind is given this last opportunity to hear it, repent and turn to Him. This underlines God's mercy.

Angel 2
Verse 8
The second angel foretells the fall of Babylon, Babylon being the one-world system that has enabled the Antichrist to become so powerful. Although the harlot (the harlot is the state-enforced religion, which is present in the first half of the Tribulation) is destroyed mid-Tribulation (chapter 17), the political and commercial aspects continue, until they too are destroyed in the 7th bowl of wrath.

Angel 3
Verses 9-13
The third angel condemns those who follow the beast and warns against accepting the mark of the beast for there is torment and suffering for those who do. God's people are advised to endure persecution patiently to the end. All those who die in the Lord will be blessed and rewarded.

Set 2: These angels call for action to bring in the Harvest

Verse 14
In this verse we see that:

- the Son of Man sitting on a cloud is Jesus
- the white cloud denotes purity
- the gold crown denotes victory
- the sickle denotes authority

Verses 15-20
The second set of angels all come from the Temple in heaven.

Angel 4
Verses 15-16
This angel announces the wheat harvest (the harvest of believers) and tells Jesus that it is time to bring in the harvest. Jesus does this and the whole earth is harvested.

Angel 5
Verse 17

The 5th angel is deployed to be ready to harvest the grapes. He also has a sharp sickle and is sent from the Temple in heaven.

Angel 6
Verse 18

This angel has power to destroy and shouts to Angel 5 to swing his sickle because the time has come to harvest the grapes.

Verses 19-20

Angel 5 reaps the grapes. The grapes represent the armies of Antichrist at the Battle of Armageddon that are ripe for judgement. Jesus will save His people, Israel (see Isaiah 63:1-6 below).

> [1] Who is this who comes from Edom,
> from the city of Bozrah,
> with his clothing stained red?
> Who is this in royal robes,
> marching in his great strength?
>
> "It is I, the Lord, announcing your salvation!
> It is I, the Lord, who has the power to save!"
>
> [2] Why are your clothes so red,
> as if you have been treading out grapes?
>
> [3] "I have been treading the winepress alone;
> no one was there to help me.
> In my anger I have trampled my enemies
> as if they were grapes.
>
> In my fury I have trampled my foes.
> Their blood has stained my clothes.
> [4] For the time has come for me to avenge my people,
> to ransom them from their oppressors.
>
> [5] I was amazed to see that no one intervened
> to help the oppressed.
> So I myself stepped in to save them with my strong arm,
> and my wrath sustained me.
> [6] I crushed the nations in my anger
> and made them stagger and fall to the ground,
> spilling their blood upon the earth."

Map 4 showing the position of Edom, Moab and Megiddo

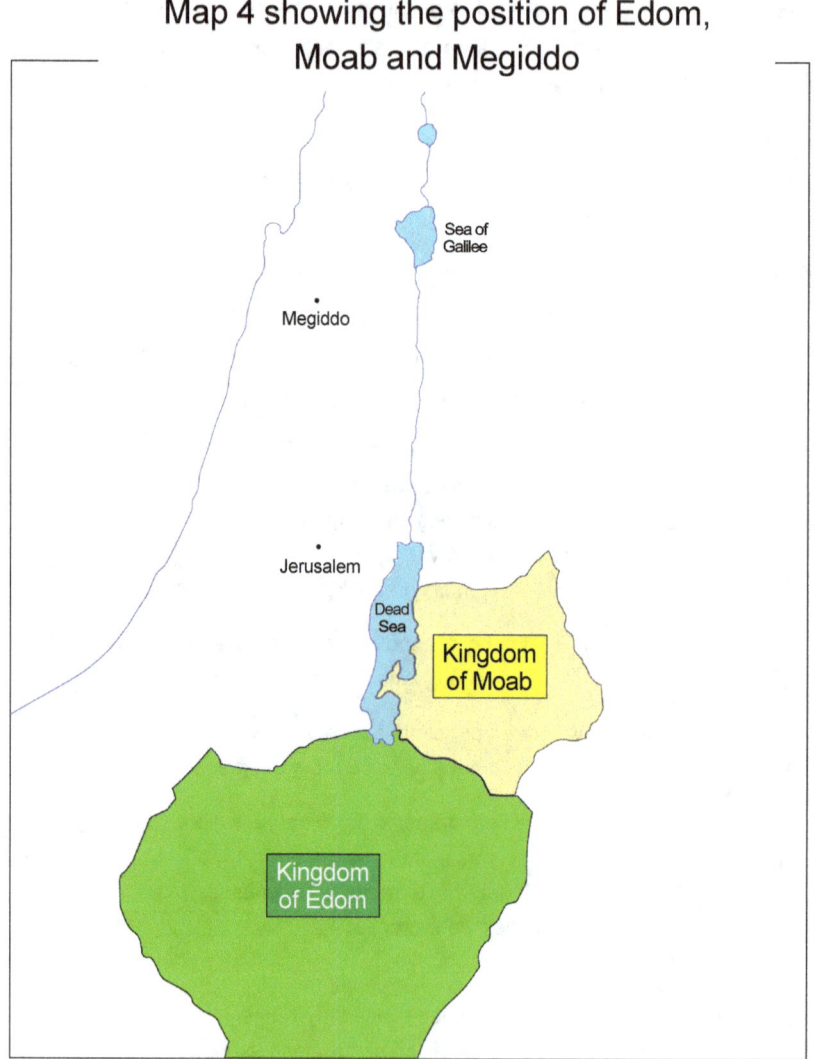

Edom is a place, south of the Dead Sea. Esau was Abraham's grandson and Isaac's son. He made this land his kingdom. Esau was not on the best of terms with his twin brother, Jacob. Jacob (renamed by God as Israel) and Esau had little to do with each other.

Both the Moabites and the Edomites became King David's servants during David's conquests, recorded in 2 Samuel 8:1-14 and 1 Chronicles 18:1-13. Many Christians think that the Messianic Jews and Christians who leave Israel at mid-Tribulation will move here for shelter.

The Book of Revelation
Chapter 15
Setting the scene for the last 7 Judgements

Background

This chapter is a preview of the things that will happen in chapter 16.

The scene is set for the final 7 judgements. The 7 bowls of judgement are contained within the 7th Trumpet. However, first of all, we see the picture of all those who have been victorious over the beast and his statue (the 'abomination of desolation' is referenced in the introduction to chapter 14).

Commentary on chapter 15

Verse 1	The vision that John sees is a heavenly one, i.e. it is what he sees happening in heaven. It is giving us a picture of the victory and rewards ahead. The rejoicing he sees must fill us all with hope for the Jews and Christians who will live during the Tribulation.
	There are 7 angels who hold the last 7 plagues that will complete God's wrath against His enemies. The Greek word for *completion* is the same as that used by Jesus on the cross when He said, "It is finished." (John 19:30).
Verse 2	Sea usually represents people, so here it represents a vast number of people. Those who had been victorious over the beast by not worshipping him were martyred for their Christian faith. In this verse we see them worshipping God as they sing a song of victory.
Verses 3-4	The song is a mixture of a song of Moses and one of Jesus, thus blending the Law and Love. The song praises God for who He is and tells us that God's works and ways honour Him and His judgements are just and righteous.

Verses 5-8

We now approach the worst part of God's judgement upon the earth. The heavenly Temple is thrown open wide. The angels are wearing robes of white, which some commentators believe are studded with jewels. They have come from priestly ministry to their current role. The gold sash denotes the livery of Jesus. The fact that the angels came from the Temple in heaven underlines the fact that these judgements are sent from God. The fact that one of the living beings who surround the throne gives a bowl to each of the 7 angels, reveals to us that God has sanctioned these judgements.

The smoke emanates from God's glory and power.

N.B. The judgements to come are severe but we need to remember that they are sent to a rebellious people with the intent that more of them should turn to Him.

> As surely as I live, says the Sovereign Lord, I take no pleasure in the death of wicked people. I only want them to turn from their wicked ways so they can live. Turn! Turn from your wickedness, O people of Israel! Why should you die? (Ezekiel 33:11)

The 7th trumpet continues to blow until all the bowls of the wrath of God's judgement have concluded, i.e. until the end of the Tribulation.

The Book of Revelation
Chapter 16
Judgements of the 7 Bowls

Commentary on chapter 16

Verse 1	The bowls of God's wrath are poured out over the earth by the 7 angels. Bowls 1-6 are poured in rapid succession.
Bowl 1 verse 2	The 1st bowl is poured on the earth. People erupt in ugly, foul sores (cf. the 6th plague of Egypt – Exodus 9:9-10). God's people will not be subject to this plague. The fact that God's people are not smitten by the plague should cause men to repent and turn to God, but it does not.
Bowl 2 verse 3	The 2nd bowl is poured on the sea. All living things in the sea die. This is similar to, but more severe than, Trumpet 2 (chapter 8). There is a foul smell of death and decay.
Bowl 3 verses 4-7	The 3rd bowl is poured on all fresh-water rivers and streams and they become blood. This is similar to, but more severe than, Trumpet 3 (chapter 8). The angel of the waters, who is dispensing Bowl 3, leaves us in no doubt that this judgement is sent because of the martyring of God's holy people, including the prophets. The angel heralds this as a just judgement for the crimes committed (cf. the 1st plague of Egypt – Exodus 7:14-21).

Another angel, calling from the altar, affirms that God's judgements are righteous and true. |
| **Bowl 4** verses 8-9 | The 4th bowl is poured onto the sun. Despite this dreadful period of being scorched by the sun (also referred to in Isaiah 24:6, Isaiah 42:25 and Malachi 4:1), people still refuse to turn to God. |

Jesus tells us that, unless these times are shortened, no one will be saved from perishing. (Matthew 24:22).

Bowl 5
Verses 10-11

The 5th bowl is poured onto the throne of the beast and his kingdom. There is a time of darkness. (Isaiah 60:2 speaks of great darkness before the glory of the Lord appears.)

Still, people do not repent.

Bowl 6
Verses 12-16

The 6th bowl is poured onto the great Euphrates River. This begins the preparation for the Battle of Armageddon. *Ar* means *hill* so *Armageddon* means *Hill of Megiddo*, the hill of slaughter (see Map 4).

The waters of the River Euphrates dry up. Consequently, there is now no border between the East and the Land of Israel.

Following this there is a pause before the outpouring of Bowl 7 so that various things can happen.

1. Three demonic spirits, pictured as frogs, come from the mouths of the dragon, the beast and the false prophet. These demonic spirits entice the armies of the countries of the East and Far East to send troops into Israel.

2. These troops will gather on the Hill of Megiddo, which is in the north of Israel and overlooks the Jezreel Valley, which is vast and very flat; an ideal place for troops to gather.

3. The battle is between the Antichrist's troops and Israel. It is during this battle that the Jews finally repent and all of them accept Jesus as their Saviour.

Bowl 7
Verses 17-20

The 7th bowl is poured into the air.

These judgements, which again come from the Temple in heaven, happen towards the end of the Battle of Armageddon†, shortly before Christ returns.

The earthquake, greater than any before it, destroys all the cities of the world including Babylon because of its sin (Babylon is associated with the Antichrist). The splitting of Babylon into 3 implies that the Antichrist's whole empire is destroyed (cf. Joel 2:30-31 and Revelation 6:12-17). The hail stones, that are part of the terrifying storm that accompanied the earthquake, are large enough to kill (cf. Ezekiel 38:20-23).

Do people now repent? No! Instead, they curse God!

The Book of Revelation
Chapter 17
Babylon 1: Destruction of the Harlot

The harlot is destroyed in the middle of the Tribulation.

Chapters 17 and 18 are both part of the same topic: Babylon. Chapter 17 relates more to the spiritual Babylon, while chapter 18 refers to the political and economic Babylon.

Background to Babylon

Noah's great grandson, Nymrod (which means *rebellious one*), seems to have been the instigator of the rebellion against God by the people of Babel. These people built an enormously tall tower where they could worship the sun, moon and stars (Genesis 11:1-9). The name *Babel* means *for themselves*. It is thought that occult traditions began here. It is also believed that this is where Babylon originated.

Introduction

In chapter 17, Babylon is described as a toxic combination of religious, political and economic power.

The harlot	represents the apostate church. This false church is the antithesis of the true church.

The true church is the bride of Christ.

The beast	refers to the political power.

The harlot sits on the beast – this creates a state religion which, in whatever form it appears, is not true Christianity and it is controlled by the Antichrist.

Commentary on Chapter 17

Verses 1-6	Describe the harlot and her multitude of sins; e.g. idolatry, blasphemy against God, persecution of the Jewish nation and of Christians, and immorality

(cf. chapter 14:8). The time has come for her to be judged for her sins.

The *many waters* indicates that multitudes of people from all nations belong to this apostate religion.

Verses 7-8 Retell the destruction of the beast and his coming alive again. All people who have not chosen Jesus as their Saviour will be amazed. These people will not have their names in the Lamb's Book of Life (cf. Revelation 13:3 and 8).

Verses 9-10 The political beast on which she, the harlot, sits has 7 heads. These represent 7 successive world empires, their chronological order being:

1st Egypt
2nd Assyria
3rd Babylon
4th Persia
5th Greece
6th Rome
7th The world empire at the time of the Tribulation.

Five of these empires had already fallen when John wrote the Book of Revelation (Daniel 2:31-45).

The Roman Empire, the 6th empire, was actually in power at the time of Jesus and beyond (31 BC to 476 AD).

The 7th head is the world empire in the time of the Tribulation. The 10 horns (on the 7th head) are the 10 kings who, at first, will reign under the Antichrist during the Tribulation.

Verse 11 The 8th head is the scarlet beast (also known as the beast of the sea or the Antichrist). He is the same beast that was dead and became alive again

	(Revelation 13:3-4). He is directed and empowered by Satan.
Verse 12	The 10 horns are 10 leaders who will rule with the Antichrist for a brief period of time.
Verses 13-14	The beast and the 10 kings wage war against Jesus and His followers but Jesus defeats them as He is King of kings and Lord of lords.
Verses 15-18	At mid-Tribulation, the harlot (the apostate church) is killed, destroyed by the Antichrist for he has no further need of her. At this point, the Antichrist becomes the world power who, together with the false prophet, institutes his own religion: worshipping the beast, i.e. himself.

The Book of Revelation
Chapter 18
Babylon 2: Final Destruction of political Babylon

The timing of this chapter is towards the end of the Tribulation.

Nations who will fight against Israel in the Battle of Armageddon

In Ezekiel 38:1-9, we discover the identity of the nations who will fight against Israel at the Battle of Armageddon. In these verses, Gog means a king or prince. There is no exact correlation between the boundaries of kingdoms referred to in Ezekiel and boundaries of modern day countries. We, therefore, find some modern day countries appearing more than once.

Ezekiel 38:1-9	**Refers to modern day…**
Rosh	Russia
Magog	Central Asia and part of Russia
Meshech	Part of Turkey
Tubal	Part of Turkey, Southern Russia and part of Iran
Persia	Iran
Ethiopia	Sudan
Put	Libya
Gomer	Part of Turkey
Beth – Togarmah	Part of Turkey

Magog, Tubal and Mesheck are tribes descending from Noah's 2nd, 5th and 6th sons, respectively. These have been verified by finds from many archaeological digs.

Commentary on chapter 18

Verse 1 Another angel, who displays the authority and splendour given to him by God, announces the final destruction of the Babylonian world system. This is a necessary judgement because of the rebellion of Babylon against God, which led to such things as:

- immoral behaviour

- an infestation of demonic powers
- gross corruption
- overindulgence in extravagant luxury
- and, most particularly, persecution of God's people (verse 20)

This mighty empire needs to be dealt with in its entirety and removed completely from God's new world order in the Millennium.

Verse 4	A warning is given to God's people to separate themselves from the ways of this Babylonian empire; they are to live in the world and not be of it but remain true to God and all His ways.
Verses 5-7	The enormity of Babylon's sins is listed together with her gloating comments and boast of being queen and untouchable.
Verses 8-10	Because of her pomposity and sin, this Babylonian empire will be destroyed speedily by earthquake, fire and plague. Thus, God will judge her in a single day!
Verses 11-17a	All the merchants who became rich on Babylon's gluttony for luxury are in mourning for they no longer have a market for their luxury goods. They seem to be in disbelief that Babylon has been destroyed so quickly.
Verses 17b-19	Similarly, the merchant ship crews, who have been transporting all these goods, will mourn their loss of income.
Verses 20-24	However, heaven rejoices at the judgement of Babylon. At last, Babylon has been judged for the sake of all God's people, apostles and prophets. The millstone thrown into the sea denotes the fact that Babylon will indeed be totally destroyed, never to rise again.

The Book of Revelation
Chapter 19
Jesus' Second Coming

Commentary on chapter 19

Heaven erupts in loud and mighty songs of praise, as God has punished the great prostitute (also known as the harlot and the apostate church) and avenged the murder of His people. Jesus is about to return at His second coming and complete this phase of His work. All enemies will be overcome and judged and the earth will be released from the bondage of sin.

The chapter commences with Alleluias in heaven.

Alleluia 1 Verses 1-2	Praise for who God is and what He has done in securing the salvation of mankind and the world and in punishing the great prostitute†.
	Praise for His true and righteous judgements in judging the harlot† and avenging the death of God's people at her hand.
Alleluias 2-3 Verses 3-4	As smoke rises in heaven signifying the power of God, the 24 elders and the 4 beasts fall down and worship God with alleluias and an amen.
Alleluia 4 Verses 5-6	After an invitation from the throne, all of God's servants are able to join in with thunderous praise saying, "Alleluia, for the Lord God, the Almighty, reigns."
Verses 7-9	The bride (the Church) is presented to Jesus. Now Jesus is preparing to take control of the world.

The Rider on the White Horse.

Verse 11	The rider, as you might expect, is Jesus, the Word of God (John 1:1). The horse signifies a warrior king: mighty, powerful and victorious. Jesus is described as

judging fairly. The war to come will, therefore, be a righteous war.

Verse 12	Jesus' eyes are flames of fire, i.e. all-seeing, as He brings judgement on all the earth. Nothing will be left unrevealed to Him. Jesus is crowned with the crowns of all the world's kingdoms. The Greek word for *crown* here (*diadema*) means *kingly crown* as opposed to the beast's laurel one.
Verse 13	His clothing is dipped in blood and He is given the title, *Word of God* (cf. John 1:1).
Verse 14	The armies of heaven will ride with Him. They are on white horses and they wear white. These armies are generally thought to be either the bride of Christ (the Church) wearing white (verses 7-8), or angels.
Verse 15	The sharp, two-edged sword is used to strike down the enemies of God, who will gather against Him at the Battle of Armageddon. We are also told that 'the Word of God is sharper than any two-edged sword' (Hebrews 4:12).
	Jesus will release God's fierce anger and crush these enemies and the blood from the battle will stain Jesus' garments. This will be similar to the way a person who has been treading grapes is stained with grape juice. However, the stains on Jesus' clothes are from the blood of His enemies, not grape juice.
Verse 16	The title *King of kings and Lord of lords* is written both on Jesus' clothes and also on His thigh.
Verses 17-21	The sharp sword that came out of Jesus' mouth kills the entire army. Because of the carnage following this battle, an angel calls vultures to eat

	the flesh of the men and animals that now lie strewn across the land.
Verse 20	The beast (the Antichrist) and the false prophet are captured and thrown into the sulfurous, burning lake.

The battle has ended.

The Tribulation is over.
There is no more need for the 7th Trumpet so it has fallen silent.

Jesus has won the victory.

The Book of Revelation
Chapter 20
The Millennium

Background

Preparations for the millennial reign:

- The establishment of a 'theocratic monarchy'† with Jesus as King and God's people in roles of authority in His kingdom.
- Geographical and structural changes in Israel, including a new millennial Temple (Ezekiel 40:5-47 & 43:1-19). A river will be released to flow south from the Temple to Jerusalem and then east and west via the newly created valley brought about by the splitting of the Mount of Olives. Flowing to the east, the river will reach the Dead Sea, which will become fresh water. Flowing west, the river will reach the Mediterranean Sea (Ezekiel 47:1-12). In addition, the earth will also be restored to how it was at the beginning of God's creation.
- Jews who have survived the Tribulation will be gathered to Israel.

The Millennium – the thousand year reign

>Jesus establishes His kingdom on earth and reigns here for 1,000 years.

>Currently, Christians hold differing views about His kingdom and reign; here are 3 of them:

1. Amillennial view:

    >This is just symbolic and there will be, therefore, no literal 1,000 year reign.

2. Post Millennial view:

    >Christ returns after the 1,000 years that follow the Tribulation.

3. Pre-Millennial view:

    Christ returns at the end of the Tribulation and reigns for a literal 1,000 years.

    Most evangelical Christians hold the pre-Millennial view.

Commentary on Chapter 20

Verses 1-3   John sees in a vision, an angel (not Jesus, probably Michael) who comes armed with a heavy chain and the key to the abyss (otherwise known as the bottomless pit). Here the worst demons are kept until the end of Christ's 1,000 year reign. The angel is given authority to bind Satan (also known as the devil or the old serpent). The angel throws him into the abyss and locks the door. Satan will remain here for the duration of the 1,000 years so that he cannot deceive people any more during this time.

The First Resurrection

Verse 4   Those on the thrones in heaven are the pre-Tribulation, raptured believers and Old Testament saints who have been given authority to judge the world, serving under Jesus (cf. 1 Thessalonians 4:15- 18).

Those who have been martyred during the Tribulation for their testimony about Jesus and their refusal to take the mark of the beast will also reign with Christ.

Chronology of those in the First Resurrection

First, Jesus at His resurrection on Easter Day
↓
Second, the Church and the Old Testament saints at the Rapture
↓
Third, those Christians who died or were martyred during the Tribulation
↓
Fourth, Christians who survived the Tribulation and continue into the Millennium and those born during the Millennium who become Christians.

Verses 5-6	For people who have come through the Tribulation, life will continue. However, there will be one monarch, Jesus, and no more political power.
	Life will be lived without the evil and deception of Satan. However, man still has a fallen nature owing to Adam and Eve's rebellion in the Garden of Eden, so there will still be sin in the world among the survivors of the Tribulation but less evil because Satan is locked in the abyss.
	Old Testament prophecies tell us how it will be during this time. Here are a few:
Isaiah 2:1-4	A time of peace when worshippers can go up to the Mount of the Lord.
Isaiah 11:1-9	A time of fair, just and righteous rule. A time when wild animals become tame and live in peaceful co-existence with man.
Isaiah 65:20-22	A time of longevity – some commentators believe that it will be unusual for a person to die before the age of 100 and, indeed, 100 will be considered

	to be young! Some may live to be 1,000.
Verse 7	After the 1,000 years of living in eutopia, Satan will be released from the abyss. This is necessary since all those who have been born during the Millennium have had no choice of allegiance. Their time of choice has now arrived and they can either choose Jesus or join the rebels and choose Satan.
	On his release, Satan will gather these rebels to himself.
Verses 8-9	*Gog* and *Magog* refer to the final rebellion against God, mentioned in verse 9. (These are not the same as the princes in Ezekiel 38 mentioned in chapter 18 of this book.) Great numbers like the sands of the sea will follow Satan from all over the world and they will form an army that will surround Jerusalem. However, fire will come down from heaven and consume them.
Verse 10	Finally, the devil (or Satan or the old serpent) will be thrown into the sulfurous lake of fire to join the beast (the Antichrist) and the false prophet.

The Great White Throne

Verses 11-15	After this, Jesus will sit on His white throne and judge the nations. Jesus speaks of this time in His parable of the sheep and the goats. The sheep (believers) will inherit the kingdom and live with Jesus forever.

The Second Resurrection (all unbelievers)

The goats, however, are both those unbelievers who are alive and those who have died (as death and Hades† will give up their dead). This is the second resurrection.

The books containing all the deeds of each individual will be opened and they will be judged accordingly.

The Lamb's Book of Life is also present. Some believe that everyone was originally entered into this book but anyone who has chosen to rebel against God has had their name blotted out of this book.

Finally, all of the unbelievers whose names are *not* written in The Lamb's Book of Life are thrown into the Lake of Fire and will remain there for eternity.

The Book of Revelation
Chapter 21
The New Jerusalem

Overview of the chapter

In this chapter, we are assured that Jesus, the Alpha and Omega has finished His work, therefore:

- all evil has been dealt with, once and for all.
- a new heaven and earth has been created.
- there will be no more sorrow or suffering in the New Jerusalem, as God has dealt with all our sorrows and wiped away our tears.
- God will dwell (He will tabernacle†) with us there in a place of perfect love and joyful existence.
- it will be a place of beauty, shining with the light of God's glory.
- all believers (the bride of Christ) throughout the ages will be present.

Commentary on Chapter 21

Verse 1	A completely new heaven and earth have been created and the first heaven and earth have gone.
Verse 2	John sees the new city of Jerusalem coming down from heaven. The city is likened to a bride who is radiant on her wedding day because the city is inhabited by all believers, both Messianic Jews† and Gentiles, from all periods of history, who are the glorified bride of Christ.
Verses 3-5	These verses emphasise that God will dwell with men for eternity in a kingdom that holds no more pain or fear or torment or sorrow or death because these things have been dealt with by Jesus and are now a thing of the past, never to return, for He has made all things new.

Verses 6-7	The phrase *I am the Alpha and Omega* tells us that this is Jesus speaking. He has completed all things. Our desire will be totally focused on the Lord and, as we thirst for more of Him, we shall be freely given our desire, through the ministrations of the Holy Spirit, Who is the Fountain of Life.
	All who believe will be in a Father-son or Father-daughter relationship with God.
Verse 8	Emphasises the fact that, in this new heaven and earth, there will be no place for the wicked, who have been judged and will remain for eternity in the sulfurous, fiery lake (Revelation 20:14).
Verse 9	One of the 7 angels, who had previously held one of the 7 Bowls of Judgement, shows John the new city of Jerusalem, which comes from heaven.
	This angel also shows John the bride of Christ.
	As we saw earlier, the bride of Christ refers to all believers throughout history.
Verses 10-11	The New Jerusalem shines and sparkles with the Glory of God. This is where the groom (Jesus) and His bride (the Church) live. With our limited vocabulary, it is difficult to describe what John saw. An insufficient description might be: 'The glory of God will shine forth from Jesus, through His bride, like brilliant, glittering multi-faceted precious stones that take our breath away.'

Verses 12-17	The city is enormous (1,400 cubic miles) and has large gates made from 12 single pearls.

A couple of other things struck me; these relate to the importance of the Jewish nation:

1. The gates bear the names of the 12 tribes of Israel (see page 21).

2. The foundation stones of the walls have the names of the 12 apostles written on them. They had witnessed to Jesus' life, work and identity as God's son, after He ascended to heaven (Acts 1:9-11). From their witness, the Church was born.

Verses 18-20	• The city itself is made of transparent gold and jasper.
	• The walls were inlaid with precious stones – jasper (clear), sapphire (blue), agate (greenish), emerald (green), onyx (white, layered with red), carnelian (fiery red), chrysolite (golden yellow), beryl (green), topaz (greenish yellow), chrysoprase (gold green), jacinth (violet) and amethyst (purple).
Verse 21	The 12 gates (3 on each side of the city wall) are made from 12 enormous pearls.

The main street is clear, pure gold. Gold represents the divine nature.

Verses 22-23	The Lord God Almighty and the Lamb are both the Temple and the glorious light of the New Jerusalem.

Verses 24-27   The city gates will constantly be open so that people of all nations can enter at any time to bring their glory and honour into the city. It will be a cosmopolitan city. Only those whose names are written in The Lamb's Book of Life may enter and they will be completely saved and accepted in the Beloved (cf. Ephesians 1:6 AV).

The Book of Revelation
Chapter 22
It is finished

The description of the New Jerusalem, which began in chapter 21, is completed when an angel speaks to John in verses 1-5.

Commentary on chapter 22

Verse 1	We see again (cf. Revelation chapter 4) the picture of the Holy Spirit (the Water of Life) flowing, as a river, from the Father, through the Son (the Lamb) and out from the throne. Believers, now in the New Jerusalem, can drink freely the Water of Life.
	Some commentators see the water as actual water, some as the Holy Spirit, while a third group believe it is a combination of both: actual water with a symbolic reference to the Holy Spirit.
Verse 2	The river flows down the centre of the main street. On each side of the river is a tree. (Some commentators believe there is only one tree, while others believe there are two or more trees.)
	The purpose of the tree(s) is twofold:
	1. Fruit for those in the city to eat.
	2. Health-giving leaves. The word for healing here means health-giving. Healing will no longer be required as we have been told that there will be no more pain or sickness as these things have already been dealt with and done away with.
Verses 3-4	The curse has been removed from everything by Jesus' sacrificial death on the cross. We shall be there worshipping God in an intimate way as we shall see His face and His name will be on our foreheads as He has claimed us for His own.

Verse 5	As we saw in chapter 21, there will be no need of any light source, apart from the glory of God. We shall reign with God forever, bathed in His love and light, each individual totally fulfilled, in the intimate relationship with Him that He had purposed from the beginning.
Verse 6	The angel assures John that all the things he has seen and heard are faithful and true: a prophecy sent from God, Who also inspired the Old Testament prophets.
Verse 7	*Jesus is speaking.* Some commentators believe that the words *soon* or *quickly* used here are better translated as *suddenly*.
Verses 8-9	John is so overcome that he wants to worship the angel. However, the angel assures John that he is just a servant and the only One to be worshipped is God.
Verses 10-11	John is advised not to seal up this prophecy because the time for them to be fulfilled is near. Before Jesus returns and the prophecy is fulfilled, man will have had the choice of turning to Him or continuing down the path of their rebellion and evil doings. When Christ has returned, they will have lost their window of opportunity, but believers will live on in God's new heaven and earth.
Verse 12	*Jesus is speaking.* The deeds spoken of here are the good things we have done during our earthly life. These have been made possible through the enabling of His Holy Spirit and brought about because of our desire to love and serve God. (Our sins have already been dealt with by Jesus on the cross.)
Verse 13	Jesus assures us that He is the Alpha and Omega, the Beginning and the End.

Verses 14-15	Only those who have believed that Jesus alone has bought their salvation (i.e. 'they have washed their robes in the blood of the Lamb' – Revelation 7:14b) will be in this new Jerusalem. Depraved mankind, who love evil, will have already been dealt with and thrown into the lake of fire.
Verse 16	*Jesus is speaking.* The reference to Jesus as being both the source of David and the heir to his throne may seem like a paradox at first but it is easily explained by the facts that:

- Jesus was with God at the beginning of creation. (In Genesis 1:1, the word for *Godhead* is plural – *Elohim*). Jesus being a part of the Godhead was there at the beginning of creation – so He is the source of David.

- Jesus was born of David's line and so is a descendent of David. (Isaiah 11:1-5,10)

> [1] Out of the stump of David's family will grow a shoot—
> yes, a new Branch bearing fruit from the old root.
> [2] And the Spirit of the Lord will rest on him—
> the Spirit of wisdom and understanding,
> the Spirit of counsel and might,
> the Spirit of knowledge and the fear of the Lord.
> [3] He will delight in obeying the Lord.
> He will not judge by appearance
> nor make a decision based on hearsay.
> [4] He will give justice to the poor
> and make fair decisions for the exploited.
> The earth will shake at the force of His word,
> and one breath from his mouth will destroy the wicked.
> [5] He will wear righteousness like a belt
> and truth like an undergarment.

> [10] In that day the heir to David's throne
> will be a banner of salvation to all the world.
> The nations will rally to Him,
> and the land where He lives will be a glorious place.

Jesus also calls Himself the Bright Morning Star. There is a very bright star that shines at the darkest part of the night, shortly before dawn. This title reminds us that, at the darkest time in the history of mankind, Jesus will come to bring His light into the world and the dark times will then be gone for ever.

Verse 17	Some commentators think that this verse refers to

1. A time before Jesus' return: the Holy Spirit and the bride (the Church) are telling Jesus to come. All who are on earth and have not committed themselves to God, but want to, are encouraged to drink of the Water of Life and come to Him and also

2. The New Jerusalem: anyone can come to the Water of Life and be satisfied.

Other commentators believe that this verse refers to only post millennial existence. The verse tells us to "come" and speaks of the freedom we shall have to partake of the Water of Life whenever we desire to do so.

Verses 18-19	Give a solemn warning of the consequences that will happen if anyone tries to add or take away from the words of the prophecy of the Book of Revelation.
Verse 20	Jesus tells us He is coming soon and the response is, "So be it; come Lord Jesus."
Verse 21	The book ends with a blessing of God's grace to all who are His people.

"Blessing and honour and glory and power

be unto Him that sitteth upon the throne

and unto the Lamb for ever and ever."

(Revelation 5:13b)

The End

Appendix 1

Jesus' Olivet Discourse

What Jesus said regarding the Tribulation and His Second Coming

Matthew 24:2

Jesus speaks of the destruction of the 2nd Temple:

> "Do you see all these buildings? I tell you the truth, they will be completely demolished. Not one stone will be left on top of another!"

This happened in AD 70 when the Romans destroyed the Temple during the siege of Jerusalem.

This was the Temple completed in 516 BC by those who returned from captivity in Babylon. It was the second Temple to be built on that site and Herod the Great reconstructed and enlarged it some time between 74 and 4 BC. The first Temple was Solomon's Temple, which was destroyed when the Israelites were taken into captivity in 586 BC.

This is important because there has been no third temple built in Jerusalem. This will happen when the Antichrist rears his head and makes a treaty with Israel.

The Tribulation

Verses 7-8	Jesus describes the start of the Tribulation as birth pangs, although there is much pain, destruction, war, earthquakes (see notes on Seals 1-6).
Verse 14	There will be worldwide preaching of the Gospel and then the end will come. We know that the Gospel is preached throughout the Tribulation, spearheaded by the 144,000 Jewish Christians sent out at the beginning of the Tribulation (Revelation 7:4-8).

Mid-Tribulation

Verse 15	Jesus tells of the sign mid-Tribulation when He speaks of the abomination of desolation†, which is set up in the Temple (also prophesied by Daniel in Daniel 9:27).
Verse 16	At this point, Jews in Jerusalem and the surrounding area need to flee to the hills.

(Most commentators believe that a period of about 30 days will be available for them to flee before the start of the last 3½ years, which comprise The Great Tribulation, when the Antichrist is empowered by Satan to wreak havoc and introduces the mark of the beast.)

The Great Tribulation

Verse 22	This period in history will be so bad that, unless God intervenes, no one will survive. God does so for the sake of those remaining who belong to Him.

Signs that the Second Coming is near

Matthew 24:4-6	[4]Jesus told them, "Don't let anyone mislead you, [5]for many will come in my name, claiming, 'I am the Messiah.' They will deceive many. [6] And you will hear of wars and threats of wars, but don't panic. Yes, these things must take place, but the end won't follow immediately.
Matthew 24:23-26	[23]"Then if anyone tells you, 'Look, here is the Messiah,' or 'There he is,' don't believe it. [24] For false messiahs and false prophets will rise up and perform great signs and wonders so as to deceive, if possible, even God's chosen ones. [25] See, I have warned you about this ahead of time. [26] "So if someone tells you, 'Look, the Messiah is out in the desert,' don't bother to go and look. Or, 'Look, he is hiding here,' don't believe it!

	Jesus warns of deceivers who will claim to be the Christ – but the end is not yet.
Luke 21:20	Armies will surround Jerusalem.
	[20] "And when you see Jerusalem surrounded by armies, then you will know that the time of its destruction has arrived."

Jesus' Second Coming

Matthew 24

Verse 36	No one knows when Jesus will return; only God the Father. He will come as a thief in the night.
Verse 23	Christ's second coming will be unlike His first. The signs before His coming will be:
Verse 29	• There will be darkness, for neither sun nor moon will give light and the stars will disappear from the sky.
	• When He comes, He will light up the whole sky, just as lightning does, only far more so.
Verse 30	• All people will see Him coming on the clouds of heaven in great power and glory.
Verse 31	• He will send out angels to gather His chosen ones from all over the world.
Verse 30	• All people on earth will mourn deeply.

Appendix 2

The relevance of the Book of Daniel to the Book of Revelation

Reproduced by kind permission of James Parks

The statue in Nebuchadnezzar's dream

Background

Daniel, a Jewish scholar, was taken captive by the Babylonians in 607 BC. He remained there until his death around 536 BC. During this time he had many prophesies.

Many of the writings and prophecies in Daniel are pertinent to the Book of Revelation. They help us to piece together the time lines and interpret some passages in the Book of Revelation.

Daniel chapter 2 (verses 19-45)

The interpretation of Nebuchadnezzar's dream about a statue of a man

The parts of the man in Nebuchadnezzar's dream represent the Gentile nations who will rule over Israel at some point in history. They are jointly referred to as Babylon.

Statue of a man

Golden head	Babylonian Empire 625-538 BC.
Silver chest and arms	Medo-Persian Empire 539-333 BC.
Bronze stomach and thighs	Greco-Macedonian Empire 333-31 BC.
Iron legs	Roman Empire 31 BC-476 AD.
Feet and toes, iron and baked clay	There are 10 powers that have political domination over Israel from 476 -1917 AD.
	The toes are the final 10 world powers that are eventually ruled over by the Antichrist.

In Nebuchadnezzar's dream the statue was struck at the feet and the whole statue was crushed into dust, which blew away in the wind. This dream depicts the total destruction of the 7 Gentile powers who will have ruled over Israel.

Daniel chapter 4

Daniel chapter 4 is important because we are introduced to the word *time* starting at verse 33. A *time* was the ancient Babylonian word for a period of 360 days (the number of days in their year). It was for 7 *times* that King Nebuchadnezzar lost his sanity and became like a beast of the field. This was a period of 7 Babylonian years.

King Nebuchadnezzar's empire was depicted by the golden head of the statue. Thus, he was the first of the 7 Gentile powers who would dominate Israel.

Daniel chapter 5

In this chapter we have the episode of the writing on the wall in the time of Belshazzar. (Belshazzar was one of Nebuchadnezzar's grandsons through his daughter, Nitocris.) The text conveys that Babylon's days were numbered and that they had been weighed in the balance and found wanting. In addition, in his book, 'The 7 Times of the Gentiles', Derek Walker sees another, underlying interpretation based on the numerical value of words. The words on the wall were *mene, mene, tekel* and *parsin*.

The basic Hebrew unit at that time was the gerah. A mina = 1,000 gerahs, a shekel = 20 gerahs and a parsin (which is ½ a mina) = 500 gerahs.

The value of *Mene* is a *mina*. The value of *Tekel* is a *shekel*.

If we consider that the gerahs are denoting years, we are left with the following interpretation of the writing on the wall.

$$
\begin{aligned}
1 \text{ Mina} &= 1{,}000 \text{ years plus} \\
1 \text{ Mina} &= 1{,}000 \text{ years plus} \\
1 \text{ Shekel} &= 20 \text{ years plus} \\
1 \text{ Parsin} &= 500 \text{ years} \\
\text{Total:} & 2{,}520 \text{ years}
\end{aligned}
$$

The writing on the wall confirms that Israel would be dominated by Gentile nations for 2,520 years.

The first wave of captured Jews from Israel was in 607 BC. Daniel was taken captive at this time.

607 BC + 2,520 years comes to 1914 AD. World War I began in 1914 and this was the beginning of the end of Gentile rule over Israel.

In 604 BC, more Israelite captives were taken to Babylon.

604 BC + 2,520 years = 1917. In 1917, the Balfour Declaration was published by the British government on 31 October. It endorsed the idea of the nation of Israel having a homeland in Palestine. On 11 December in that year, General (later Field Marshall) Allenby captured Jerusalem from the Ottoman army. These events were the beginning of Israel's move back to the land promised by God to Abraham in Genesis chapter 15:18-20 and of her once again being recognised as a nation.

Daniel chapter 7

This chapter helps us to understand the beast that came out of the sea (the Antichrist) in Revelation 13:1-2.

The meaning of 2 of the beasts recorded in the Book of Daniel:

Verse 6: **beast 3**

> The leopard represents Greece under the kingship of Alexander the Great.
> The leopard has 4 birds' wings so that it could move more speedily, and 4 heads.
> The leopard is given great authority.

Verses 7-8: **beast 4**

> Most terrifying of them all and very strong.
> It devoured and crushed victims with its iron teeth and then trampled their remains beneath its feet.

It had 10 horns and bronze claws.

A small horn with human eyes appears and 3 of the original horns are torn out to make room for it. This beast has a mouth with which it boasts.

Daniel's 4th beast represents the world power that will have dominion during the Tribulation.

The 10 horns are the same as the 10 horns of the Beast (Revelation chapters 13:1-2 and 17:3).
The 10 horns are 10 leaders who will rule the last empire until the Antichrist becomes leader of them all.

Verses 20-22   describe the Antichrist.

Verses 23-26   prophesy about the actions of the Antichrist but tell us that God will intervene and completely destroy him.

Verses 13-14 & 27
  speak of Jesus' final reign, described in the last chapters of Revelation when God's people will reign with Him.

Daniel chapter 8

In this chapter the goat and its horn relates to the history of the Grecian Empire, culminating in a description of Antiochus Epiphanes, who is a 'type'† of the Antichrist.

The goat   represents Greece.

The horn   represents Alexander the Great.

Verses 8-9 & 21   Xerxes, a Persian, was thwarted in his attempt to conquer lands to the west as Alexander the Great moved his army to attack with great speed. (This corresponds to the wings of the leopard – see beast 3.)

Verse 22	When Alexander died, the empire was divided among 4 generals (the 4 horns).

- Cassander took the European section (Macedonia and Greece).
- Lysimachus took Asia Minor (Turkey).
- Seleucus took Asia – all the eastern part of the empire except Egypt.
- Ptolemy took Egypt and North Africa.
  Daniel is told that the vision of the ram and the goats pertain to the very end times.

Verse 9	The little horn, which comes from one of the small horn powers above is Antiochus Epiphanes of the Seleucid line that took Syria. (Daniel chapter 11). He is a picture of the Antichrist who appears during the end times.
Verse 26	Daniel is assured that these things will not happen for a very long time, so he was told to keep them secret.

Daniel chapter 9

This chapter gives us an explanation of the time frame of end time† events

Verses 1-23	Daniel confesses the wickedness of Israel and that God has judged them in the way that He warned He would (e.g. in Isaiah chapter 59). Daniel pleads for mercy, not because they deserve it, but because God's nature is to be merciful. After a time, the Angel Gabriel comes to Daniel and gives him the following message.
Verse 24	[24] "A period of seventy sets of seven has been decreed for your people and your holy city to finish their rebellion, to put an end to their sin, to atone for their guilt, to bring in everlasting righteousness, to confirm the prophetic vision, and to anoint the Most Holy Place.

A period of 70 sets of 7 is given as the time span for the Jews to finish their rebellion and atone for their guilt.

> The word for **set** or **weeks** is **shabua**, which means a unit of measure with a value of 7. Daniel is, therefore, referring to 70 x 7 units of time.
>
> While Daniel was in captivity in Babylon, he was reading the prophesies of Jeremiah, who was living in Jerusalem. Jeremiah spoke in terms of years. The Jews would spend 70 years in captivity as a punishment for breaking the laws concerning sabbatical years. A sabbatical year occurred once every 7 years. During it, all land was to be left untilled and unplanted so that it had a year of rest in which to recover.

70 sabbatical years was, therefore, 70 × 7, which equals 490 years.

Verse 25
> [25] Now listen and understand! Seven sets of seven plus sixty-two sets of seven will pass from the time the command is given to rebuild Jerusalem until a ruler (the Anointed One) comes. Jerusalem will be rebuilt with streets and strong defences, despite the perilous times.

In verse 25 the period of time is recorded as:

$$7 \text{ sets of } 7 = 49 \text{ years} \quad \text{plus}$$
$$62 \text{ sets of } 7 = 434 \text{ years}$$
$$\text{therefore } 69 \text{ sets of } 7 = 483 \text{ years}$$

458 BC is the date when King Artaxerxes set out a decree that both the temple and the city walls of Jerusalem should be completed. This was in the 7th year of his reign.

458 BC + 483 years (69 sets of 7) brings us to 26 AD.

26 AD is the date when John the Baptist began his ministry.

Jesus' ministry is regarded as commencing with John the Baptist's, so Jesus' ministry consists of

```
AD 26                            AD 30                        AD 33
   | John the Baptist 3½ years  |    Jesus 3½ years          |
0 yrs.                           3½ yrs.                      7 yrs.
```

This is important to note because, in the Tribulation, Moses and Elijah witness to Jesus for 3½ years then the Antichrist rules for 3½ years. This is another Satanic parallel with God's plans.

Verse 26a "After this period of sixty-two sets of seven, the Anointed One will be killed, appearing to have accomplished nothing, and a ruler will arise whose armies will destroy the city and the Temple."

After this period of 62 sets of 7, the Messiah will be cut off, having appeared to accomplish nothing (i.e. Jesus was crucified and His people did not believe in Him).

AD 26 marks the end of the 483 years. On 3 April AD 33, Jesus was crucified. This would have been Daniel's 70th week or the last 7 years that are unaccounted for. However, since the Jews did not accept Jesus as their Messiah at that time, the Church Era began. This has enabled millions of Gentiles, as well as Jews, to become Christians. Daniel's 70th week is, therefore, now believed to be the 7 years of the Tribulation.

Verse 26b "…and a ruler will arise whose armies will destroy the city and the Temple. The end will come with a flood, and war and its miseries are decreed from that time to the very end."

This ruler is referring to 2 men: Titus, in 70 AD and the Antichrist in the second half of the Tribulation.

Verse 27	"The ruler will make a treaty with the people for a period of one set of seven, but after half this time, he will put an end to the sacrifices and offerings. And as a climax to all his terrible deeds, he will set up a sacrilegious object that causes desecration, until the fate decreed for this defiler is finally poured out on him."

This verse refers to the Antichrist, who is in power for 7 years, i.e. the duration of the Tribulation.

After the first 3½ years he reneges on his treaty with Israel and an image of the Antichrist is placed in the Temple. He then demands that all should worship him.

Daniel Chapter 11

Chapter 11 is a continuation of chapter 8 but it provides more historical detail

Verses 3-4	Refer to Alexander the Great. When he died, his empire was ruled over by 4 of his generals and their descendants. The most notable of these were the Ptolemies and the Seleucids, who were enemies.
Verse 5	The King of the South (Egypt) was ruled over by one of the Ptolemies. The King of the North (Syria) was ruled over by one of the Seleucids.
Verses 6-9	Ptolemy III Euergetes, from the south, finally made war on the Seleucids and won.
Verses 10-13	There was continual war between Egypt and Syria. Israel became a captive of first one and then the other and was treated very badly by both of them.
Verse 17	circa 198 BC. Antiochus III the Great made a treaty with Egypt and gave his daughter, Cleopatra, in marriage to Ptolemy Epiphanes.

Verse 21	Circa 175 BC, Antiochus IV Epiphanes was the vile King of Syria. He was the little horn mentioned in Daniel 8:23. He was of Seleucid descent. He was deceitful, a liar and a blasphemer (he was a 'type'† of the Antichrist).
Verse 31	In 170 BC, Antiochus killed over 100,000 Jews and took away the daily sacrifice from the temple. He also desecrated the temple with an image of Jupiter to be worshipped and for pigs' blood and broth to be offered as sacrifices on the altar (pigs were unclean animals in the Jewish religion). This was an 'abomination of desolation'† (cf. the desolation of the Temple by the Antichrist in Revelation 13:5-6).

Verses 36-45 refer to the end times.

Verse 36	Daniel now leaps forward to the end times and the Antichrist. The king is, therefore, the Antichrist. A description follows, which is covered in Revelation 13: *Background*.
Verse 40	The King of the North is thought to be Russia. The King of the South is the King of Egypt but many commentators believe that the majority, or even all of Africa, will join in the fight against the Antichrist. However, finally, in verses 42-43, they yield to him and he gains control of the gold, silver and other treasures of Egypt, Libya and Ethiopia.

Verse 41	Edom and Moab (see Map 4), in the south-east, will escape the Battle of Armageddon.
	The Tidings from the East refers to multitudes coming into Israel from the east and far east.
Verse 45	The sea referred to is the Mediterranean. The Antichrist will have his headquarters on the holy mountain (Mount Moriah) between the Mediterranean and Jerusalem. The Antichrist's rule comes to a sudden end when Jesus returns.

Daniel Chapter 12

This chapter again refers to timings of the Tribulation in the Book of Revelation.

In this chapter:

- *The people* refers to Israel.
- *In the latter days* refers to the end times.
- The vision is for *many days*, i.e. it will be a long time before this will happen.

Verse 1	This verse refers to the Tribulation, which will be brief but an intense time of trouble on earth (cf. Matthew 24:15-26). The Archangel Gabriel, who stands guard over Israel, is also mentioned in Revelation 12:7.
Verses 5-7	The length of The Great Tribulation is specified as a ***time, times*** and ***half a time***, which makes 3½ years (see notes on Daniel chapter 4 for the length of a ***time***). The last half (3½ years) of the Tribulation is often referred to as The Great Tribulation as they will be the most difficult years to live through.

Verses 8-9	Daniel is puzzled but again requested to keep the secret sealed until the 'end times'†.
Verses 10-13	Many people will become Christians during the Tribulation. The wicked will not understand what is happening but the wise will. During this second half of the Tribulation, the Jews will no longer be able to offer sacrifices to God (for 1,290 days, which equals 3½ years). Instead, the abomination that makes desolation (the image of the Antichrist) shall be set up to be worshipped there ('in the Temple' is inferred here cf. Matthew 24:15). Finally, Daniel is told that he will not live to see these times.

Glossary

Abomination of Desolation	is something that greatly defiles the Temple of God; for example the statue of the Antichrist, which was placed in the Temple of God (Revelation 13:5-6).
Antithesis	direct opposite.
Apostasy	the act of giving up one's Christian beliefs for false ones.
Apostate	false; one who has renounced their true religious faith for a false one.
Apostles	those who have been appointed and sent out by Jesus Christ.
Apostolic	to follow the ways and teachings of Jesus Christ, in the way the apostles did.
Apostolic Church	a Christian church, founded by the apostles, that continues the Biblical teaching passed down from them.
Armageddon	is the assembly point for troops on the Hill of Megiddo for the final battle before Christ returns.
Bride of Christ	is a term used by Christians as a name for the glorified Church.
End times	is the period of time just prior to Jesus' second coming.
Great Prostitute	is another name given to the Harlot or the false (apostate) church.
Hades	is the underground abode of the spirits of the dead who are awaiting the second judgement.

Harlot	is the false, state-enforced religion also known as the great prostitute, present only in the first half of the Tribulation.
Inerrancy	lack of error, infallible.
Inerrant	incapable of being wrong.
Mark of the beast	This is the mark that the Antichrist places upon all his followers, either on their forehead or their hand. It allows them to buy and sell goods, thus they are able to obtain food and essentials. Those who do not accept the mark of the beast (i.e. Jews and Christians) will not be able to do so.
Messianic Jews	Jews who have become Christians and so now believe that Jesus is their Messiah.
Millennial	the period of 1,000 years after the Battle of Armageddon, when Jesus will reign on earth before the final judgement.
Mosaic Law	the laws given by God to Moses on Mount Sinai (Exodus chapters 19-26).
Nations	synonymous with Peoples; are races of people from different geographical backgrounds.
Omniscience	God is all-knowing.
Prophecies	are messages or visions given by God to a person foretelling His future plans.
Prophetic	an accurate prediction of the future (in this case given by Yahweh).

Prophetic revelations
God-given, accurate predictions of His future plans.

Prophetic visions	supernatural dreams or pictures given by God to individuals, which accurately predict what will happen in the future.
Tabernacle	the noun means 'tent'; however, the verb, 'to tabernacle' means 'to live closely with another or others in their dwelling place.'
The Rapture	is the time when all Christian believers will rise from the earth to meet Jesus in the clouds. This will happen at some point before the Tribulation.
Theocracy	is a form of government led only by God (Yahweh) and those to whom He gives power to rule which, in this case will be the Church.
Theocratic monarchy	is a kingdom ruled by God (Yahweh).
Tribulation	A period of 7 years when life on earth will be more difficult than at any other time in history. God first withdraws His protection from the earth and then judges the evil in it.
Type	A 'type' is something (an object or a person) that foreshadows something or someone else. For example, Adam and Jesus (Romans 5:14).
Witnesses	tell people about what they have seen or heard. When people are witnesses to Satan, they deceive people into believing that he is the one to whom they should bow.
	When people are witnessing to Jesus they are giving evidence regarding His authenticity as the Son of God and Saviour of the world, so He is the One to whom they should bow.

Bibliography

Derek Walker – A Chronological commentary on the Book of Revelation

Derek Walker – Daniel's Seventy Weeks

Derek Walker – A Panorama of Prophecy

Derek Walker – The Seven Times of the Gentiles

J Vernon McGee – Through the Bible Series – The Book of Revelation

J Vernon McGee – Through the Bible Series – The Book of Ezekiel

J Vernon McGee – Through the Bible Series – The Book of Daniel

Tyndale New Testament Commentaries – The Book of Revelation

Encyclopaedia Britanica

Video Teaching

Gary Hamrick – The Book of Revelation, verse-by-verse series

Gary Hamrick – The Book of Ezekiel

www.ingramcontent.com/pod-product-compliance
Lightning Source LLC
Chambersburg PA
CBHW071213070526
44584CB00019B/3022